Thai
BIBLE

Thai

BIBLE

Jacki Passmore

Contents

Introduction

Thai is one of the world's most exciting cuisines, with flavours that leap from the plate, exotic ingredients and jewel-bright colours. Thailand is famous for its curries, based on potent pastes of galangal, lemongrass, kaffir lime, coriander and basil, along with pungent seasonings like fish sauce and shrimp paste. Chillies, black pepper, garlic, spice pastes and aromatic herbs give Thai stir-fries and noodle dishes their distinct personality.

Snacking is a way of life in this subtropical country. Food markets offer steaming bowls of soup and noodles; savoury bites from woks of smoking oil; and an endless choice of sweets. Salads also play a significant part in this complex cuisine, combining vegetables and herbs with tangy dressings.

Sit-down meals in Thailand are not separated into courses; rather dishes arrive in a steady stream, to be shared by everyone – always with rice.

Thai Basics

If you're new to Thai cooking, the best way to familiarise yourself with the ingredients you'll be using is to make a visit to the best Asian food store in your area. Spend time browsing the shelves, reading labels and asking questions. Then fill a shopping basket with some of the basics listed on the following pages. You may want to consider starting a small herb garden so you can always have some of the essential fresh ingredients to hand. With just a few pieces of kitchen equipment (see page 9), you're ready to go!

Fridge & Pantry

These days you can find most Thai staples at your local supermarket or Asian grocer. Following is a list of the most commonly used ingredients: for more information on these and more unusual ingredients, see Special Ingredients on page 246.

FRESH INGREDIENTS

Bananas – small sweet varieties like sugar or lady finger.

Basil – Greek, holy, purple, opal, etc.

Bean sprouts – keep for only a day or two in the fridge. Blanch, drain and refresh in iced water before use.

Chillies – small bird's eye chillies are very hot and are usually used whole so they don't overpower a dish and can be easily removed. Longer varieties in red, green and yellow are milder. They can be added to a dish whole or sliced, finely shredded and used as garnish, or ground into curry pastes.

Coriander – can be difficult to grow at home, but is available at most supermarkets.

Eggplants – there are numerous varieties of eggplant: pea-sized, walnut-sized, finger-shaped, long and slender, large and fat. They are generally interchangeable in recipes.

Galangal – a root similar to ginger and used to add flavour to soups and stir-fries.

Garlic – buy firm, pink-tinged bulbs rather than the bleached variety.

Ginger – pale-skinned, young ginger is best. Slice, shred, chop, grate, or use in chunks. Pickled ginger or stem ginger in syrup can be substituted in an emergency.

Kaffir lime leaves – these intensely fragrant leaves are used whole, torn or finely shredded as seasoning and garnish. Buy fresh or frozen, rather than dried. Chopped leaves are also available in jars.

Limes – smooth-skinned common limes and knobbly-skinned kaffir limes are both vital to Thai cooking: the former for juice; the latter for grated zest. Fresh is best, but keep a bottle of lime juice in the fridge for when fresh limes are not available.

Lemongrass – this herb keeps for several weeks in the fridge. Only the lower 15 cm (6 in) of the stem is used; it may be cut into chunks, slit in half, crushed or very thinly sliced.

Mushrooms – Asian mushrooms (shiitake, enoki, wood fungus) are sold fresh by the punnet. Use within 2–3 days.

Noodles – fresh rice sheets and rice noodles keep for 2–4 days after opening. Use straight from pack, or if oily rinse quickly with hot water. Do not overcook or they will fall apart. Available from Asian stores and supermarkets.

Tofu – use soft tofu in soups, and firm tofu for stir-frying, braising and deep-frying.

PANTRY ITEMS

Bamboo shoots – tinned sliced bamboo shoots.

Chilli – crushed chilli or chilli paste in a jar or tube; chilli powder and flakes.

Coconut – canned coconut milk and cream, or powdered coconut (simply add water to make coconut cream or milk); desiccated and shredded coconut.

Curry pastes – sachets or jars of red, green, yellow and

massaman (even if you enjoy making your own pastes, these are good to have on hand).

Dried shrimp – buy in small quantities and store in a tightly closed jar.

Fish sauce – this keeps well and you'll use a lot, so buy a large bottle.

Flours – cornflour and tapioca flour; rice flour.

Mushrooms and fungi – cans of straw mushrooms; dried black cloud ear (wood ear) fungus; dried shiitakes.

Noodles – dried rice stick noodles, rice vermicelli noodles, bean-thread noodles and thin egg noodles.

Nuts – skinned raw or roasted peanuts; cashews.

Oils – peanut oil and vegetable oil or light olive oil, for general cooking and stir-fries; sesame oil.

Oyster sauce – keep refrigerated after opening.

Rice – fragrant long-grain jasmine rice for steamed and fried rice; glutinous white or black rice for sticky rice.

Shrimp paste – buy as compressed blocks, dried, or in a jar. Keep tightly sealed. Dry-roast dried paste in a little aluminium foil parcel before using.

Soy sauce – light, regular and dark soy sauce.

Spices – cumin seeds, fennel seeds, coriander seeds, cardamom pods, cinnamon sticks, star anise, turmeric, cloves, sweet paprika, black pepper, ground white pepper.

Sugar – light and dark palm sugar (light for pale sauces and dressings, dark for braising and when strong flavour and colour is needed) in a jar, block or log (or use soft brown sugar); caster sugar.

Tamarind – keep a jar of tamarind paste in the fridge.

Vinegar – rice vinegar, coconut vinegar or white vinegar.

Water chestnuts – tinned (sliced or whole).

Equipment

A wok, along with a long-handled spatula, is the most important piece of kitchen equipment for cooking Thai food. In a wok you can simmer curries and toss stir-fries. A wok is also excellent for deep-frying, as the shape and size allows you to fry numerous pieces at once. A wire cake-cooling rack covered with paper towels is useful for draining fried food, while a wire-mesh scoop or slotted metal spoon can be used for retrieving food from hot oil. If you don't have a wok, you can cook curries in a standard saucepan, and stir-fries in a large non-stick frying pan.

For cooking rice you'll need a heavy-based saucepan with a tight-fitting lid, or an electric rice cooker. A large saucepan and colander are all you need for noodles. A steamer, bamboo steaming basket or metal steamer insert for a saucepan are needed for some steamed dishes.

Ordinary chef's knives can be used for preparing ingredients, although you might want to try a Chinese cleaver for cutting through bones. For grinding herbs and spices for curry pastes, use an electric coffee grinder, spice grinder, food processor with a small bowl, blender, or heavy mortar and pestle.

Cooking Rice

In Thailand, **steamed jasmine rice** is served with almost every meal. To make 4–6 serves, place 2½ cups jasmine rice in a heavy-based saucepan and shake the pan to level the rice. Add enough water to reach about 2.5 cm (1 in) above the level of the rice. Cover with a tight-fitting lid and bring quickly to the boil over high heat, then immediately turn heat down as low as possible. Cook for about 15 minutes without removing the lid or stirring the rice. Take saucepan off the heat and let sit for about 5 minutes, to allow the rice to absorb the remaining moisture. To serve, remove lid and fluff the rice with a fork.

To make 4–6 serves **sticky rice**, pour 1½ cups glutinous rice into a bowl and cover with cold water. Leave overnight to soften. Tip into a metal strainer and rinse under running cold water. Place the strainer over a saucepan of simmering water and cover with a lid or piece of aluminium foil to seal. Steam for about 25 minutes, until tender. See page 236 for a coconut rice recipe.

Nibbles & Small Dishes

Names like 'galloping horses' and 'butterflies' let you know you're in for a treat with these zingy, spicy tastes of Thailand. Serve fried nibbles hot from the oil, and dips at room temperature or lightly chilled. Crisp cakes of rice (page 17), rice crackers, and vegetable sticks are the best partners for Thai dips, but bread, bagel crisps, lavosh or warmed flatbread will do just as well.

Thai snack foods, with deliciously intermingled aromas and bright flavours, make a perfect start to any meal. In this section you'll find small dishes such as tender smoky satay, crisp golden curry puffs, coconut-coated prawns, and spicy stuffed mussels.

‹ Butterflies (page 14)

Butterflies

Makes about 24

1 small onion, quartered

1 sprig coriander, including root

150 g (5 oz) minced chicken breast

2 teaspoons light soy sauce or fish sauce

1 teaspoon oyster sauce

½ teaspoon sugar

⅓ cup finely chopped water chestnuts

3 tablespoons chopped spring onion greens

24–30 wonton wrappers or small spring-roll wrappers (thawed if frozen)

1 egg white, lightly beaten

oil for deep-frying

sweet and sour sauce, sweet chilli dipping sauce (page 243) or other dipping sauce, to serve

Place onion, coriander and chicken in a blender and grind to a paste. Add soy or fish sauce, oyster sauce and sugar, and blend. Add water chestnuts and spring onions, and pulse until crushed but not mushy.

Place a teaspoon of filling in the centre of each wrapper. Lightly brush the edges with egg white, then pinch the wrapper together around the filling to seal, leaving the edges like a frill.

Heat oil to about 160°C (320°F) in a wok. Fry the 'butterflies', about eight at a time, until golden. Remove carefully and drain on paper towels. Serve with dipping sauce on the side.

Spring Rolls

5-cm (2-in) piece dried black cloud ear (wood ear) fungus

30 g (1 oz) bean-thread vermicelli

120 g (4 oz) fresh or canned crab meat

200 g (7 oz) pork or chicken mince

1 spring onion, finely chopped

1 clove garlic, crushed

2 teaspoons fish sauce

24 small spring-roll wrappers

oil for deep-frying

chilli, garlic and vinegar dipping sauce (page 133), to serve

Soak the fungus in boiling water for 25 minutes. Soak bean-thread vermicelli in boiling water for 10 minutes, to soften.

Flake the crab meat into a bowl and remove any fragments of shell. Add pork or chicken, spring onion, garlic and fish sauce.

Drain fungus and vermicelli, and chop finely. Add to the crab mixture and use your hands to work the ingredients until smooth.

Place a spring-roll wrapper diagonally on a cutting board and place a tablespoon of the filling along the centre. Fold the bottom flap over the filling and squeeze filling into an even log shape. Fold the side flaps in, then roll up towards the top, moistening the tip with water to stick it down. Repeat with remaining wrappers and filling. >

Heat oil to 180°C (360°F) in a wok or large pan suitable for deep-frying. Deep-fry the spring rolls, in batches, until golden-brown and cooked through (about 3 minutes).

Lift out and drain well on paper towel. Serve hot with the dipping sauce.

You can replace the crab meat with extra chicken or pork. To make vegetarian spring rolls, replace all the meat with finely diced tofu.

Creamy Dip
with Crisp Rice Cakes
Khao tang na tang

Serves 4–6

1 cup (250 ml/8 fl oz) coconut milk

1½ teaspoons crushed garlic

⅓–½ teaspoon chilli paste or dried chilli flakes

2 tablespoons finely chopped onion

1 tablespoon finely chopped fresh coriander

100 g (3½ oz) pork or chicken mince

90 g (3 oz) raw prawn meat, finely chopped

1½ tablespoons (30 ml/1 fl oz) fish sauce

sugar, to taste

salt and freshly ground black pepper

rice crackers, to serve

Pour coconut milk into a wok or saucepan and add garlic, chilli, onion and coriander. Bring to the boil, then reduce heat and simmer for about 6 minutes, stirring occasionally. Add pork or chicken and the prawn meat, and simmer for 5–8 minutes, stirring, until sauce is thick and meat is cooked. Season with fish sauce, sugar, salt and pepper, adding extra chilli if you like. Serve with bought or homemade rice crackers.

To make rice cakes, leave a 1-cm (⅜-in) layer of rice on the bottom of the saucepan or rice cooker after cooking rice, and set it aside until it has dried into a firm sheet. Then peel it off and dry in the sun or in a low oven for a few hours. Break into pieces and deep-fry until crisp and golden.

Little Baskets

Makes 24

24 precooked canapé pastry cases or fried prawn crackers

1 small onion, finely diced

60 g (2 oz) chicken or pork mince

2 teaspoons sesame oil

2 tablespoons cooked corn kernels

1 tablespoon chopped fresh coriander

1 teaspoon soy sauce or fish sauce

salt and freshly ground black pepper

1 small fresh red chilli, deseeded and cut into very thin strips

coriander leaves, for garnish

Arrange the canapé cases or prawn crackers on a serving platter. (If desired, you can use a banana leaf or other large leaf to line the platter.)

Stir-fry the onion and chicken or pork in the sesame oil until meat is cooked (about 1 minute).

Add corn, chopped coriander, soy or fish sauce and a pinch of salt and pepper, and mix well.

Place a teaspoon of filling in each 'basket' and garnish with a strip of chilli and a coriander leaf.

Hot & Spicy Dip of Dried Shrimp, Pork & Tomato

Serves 6

2–3 fresh hot red chillies, deseeded and chopped

1-cm (⅜-in) piece fresh galangal or ginger, chopped

1 small onion, roughly chopped

2–3 cloves garlic, peeled

1 tablespoon dried shrimp

1 sprig fresh coriander, including root

100 g (3½ oz) finely minced pork

2 roma tomatoes, deseeded and chopped

2 tablespoons (40 ml/1½ fl oz) oil

fish sauce or salt, to taste

VEGETABLE PLATTER

12 green beans or 3 snake beans

1 cucumber

2 carrots, peeled

1 daikon (white radish), peeled

12 button mushrooms

6 walnut-sized *makhua khun* eggplants

First, prepare the vegetables. Cut beans into 4-cm (1½-in) pieces, then slice the cucumber and carrots on an angle. Cut the daikon into leaf shapes. Wipe the mushrooms with paper towel, then cut two small wedges out of each mushroom cap, to give it a cross-shape. Cut a cross into the top of each eggplant, cutting almost all the way through, then press out each quarter ('petal') to make a flower.

To make the dip, combine the chillies, galangal or ginger, onion, garlic, dried shrimp, and coriander in a food processor and grind to a paste. Add the pork and tomatoes and chop until smooth.

Heat oil in a wok, add pork mixture and 3–4 tablespoons water and stir-fry for about 5 minutes, stirring frequently, until thick and aromatic. Season to taste with fish sauce or salt and cook a few minutes longer.

Serve the dip with the platter of prepared vegetables.

To cut crisp vegetables like daikon and carrot into decorative leaf shapes, first cut the vegetable into thin slices. Then shape each slice into a narrow oval, round off one end and cut the other to a tapering point. With a vegetable carving tool or sharp knife, remove a v-shaped strip along the centre of each slice, to mimic the central rib of a leaf.

Crab & Coconut Cream Dip

Serves 6

200 ml (7 fl oz) coconut cream

1–1½ teaspoons red curry paste (page 234)

225 g (8 oz) fresh or canned crab meat, flaked

1 spring onion (white part only), very finely chopped

fish sauce and sugar, to taste

freshly squeezed lime juice

vegetable platter (page 20)

In a small saucepan, simmer the coconut cream and curry paste for 2–3 minutes, until fragrant and slightly reduced. Add crab meat and spring onion, and simmer briefly, stirring. Season to taste with fish sauce and sugar, and add a squeeze of lime juice.

Transfer dip to a shallow bowl and serve with vegetables for dipping.

Fried Tofu with Peanut Dipping Sauce

Serves 4–6

oil for deep-frying

350 g (12 oz) firm tofu, cut into 2-cm (¾-in) cubes

¾ cup (110 g/4 oz) cornflour

1 small cucumber, cubed

peanut dipping sauce (page 240)

In a wok or a pan suitable for deep-frying, heat oil to 160°C (320°F).

Coat tofu lightly with cornflour. Add half the tofu cubes to the hot oil and fry until they rise to the surface and are golden-brown (about 1½ minutes). Remove, and drain on paper towels. Fry the remaining tofu.

Serve tofu on a platter with the cubed cucumber, with the peanut sauce in a shallow bowl for dipping.

Thai Hors d'Oeuvre

Miang kham

Serves 6–10

¼ cup diced red onion

¼ cup roasted salted peanuts

¼ cup toasted shredded coconut

¼ cup diced stem ginger in syrup or crystallised ginger

¼ cup sliced Chinese sausage (Thai *kun chiang*)

2 tablespoons dried shrimp (or ½ cup crisply fried whole small prawns or shrimps)

1 large mild red or green chilli, deseeded and sliced

betel leaves (or use witlof, small Chinese cabbage or lettuce leaves), to serve

peanut dipping sauce (page 240), to serve

Place each of the ingredients (except leaves and dipping sauce) into individual small serving bowls. Place the dipping sauce in a larger serving bowl. Arrange the bowls on a serving tray lined with a paper napkin or a piece of banana leaf, with the dip in the centre. Surround the bowls with the betel leaves.

Diners take a leaf, place an assortment of ingredients onto it, add about a teaspoon of dipping sauce, then roll the leaf up and eat.

🌶 Betel leaves have a peppery taste that is rather like witlof.

Spicy Stuffed Mussels

Makes 24

24 mussels on the half shell

2 tablespoons chopped spring onion

1 clove garlic, peeled

2 thin slices fresh ginger

1 sprig fresh coriander, roughly chopped

½ teaspoon grated lime zest

1 small fresh hot red chilli, deseeded

1½ tablespoons (30 ml/1 fl oz) oil

1½ teaspoons rice flour or cornflour

½ cup (125 ml/4 fl oz) coconut cream

fish sauce and sugar, to taste

freshly ground black pepper

shredded fresh chilli and kaffir lime leaf, for garnish

Arrange the mussels in single layers in a tiered steamer.

Place spring onion, garlic, ginger, coriander, lime zest and chilli in a spice grinder or blender and grind to a paste.

Heat oil in a wok and stir-fry the herb paste for about 1 minute. Mix flour with coconut cream and pour into the wok. Simmer, stirring, for about 2 minutes, until thickened. Season to taste with fish sauce, sugar and pepper.

Place a spoonful of the coconut mixture onto each mussel, and garnish with strips of chilli and lime leaf. Steam mussels for about 5 minutes, until cooked. Serve at once.

Galloping Horses

Makes 24

1½ tablespoons (30 ml/1 fl oz)
oil

200 g (7 oz) pork mince

1½ teaspoons red curry paste
(page 234)

1 tablespoon (15 g/¾ oz) palm
sugar or soft brown sugar

1½ tablespoons crunchy
peanut butter

1½ tablespoons (30 ml/1 fl oz)
coconut cream

fish sauce, to taste

salt and ground black pepper

24 small slices honeydew
melon

shredded fresh red chilli and
small coriander leaves, for
garnish

Heat oil in a wok and stir-fry the pork and curry paste for about 2 minutes, until well cooked and all lumps have been broken up. Add sugar, peanut butter and coconut cream, and cook over medium heat, stirring continually, until well blended and aromatic. Season to taste with a few teaspoons of fish sauce and some salt and pepper – the mixture should be tangy, salty and slightly sweet. Set aside to cool.

Arrange melon on a serving platter and top each piece with a teaspoon of pork mixture. Garnish with a strip of chilli and a coriander leaf. Serve chilled.

Orange segments, slices of pear, pineapple or mango could replace the melon.

Chilli Cashews

Serves 4–8

2½ cups (625 ml/21 fl oz)
  vegetable oil

250 g (9 oz) raw cashews

2 spring onions (white part
  and half the greens), finely
  chopped

2 fresh hot red chillies,
  deseeded and finely chopped

1 teaspoon salt

Heat the oil to 180°C (360°F) in a wok or large saucepan. Add the cashews and fry until they are golden. (Do not let them brown too much, as they will continue to cook once they come out of the oil.) Carefully tip oil and cashews into a strainer set over a bowl.

Reheat the wok (don't wipe out the coating of oil) and stir-fry the spring onions and chillies until crisp. Return cashews to the wok, add salt and toss to combine.

Allow to cool before storing in an airtight container.

Corn Fritters

Serves 4–5

2 cups corn kernels (fresh, canned or frozen)

2–3 cloves garlic, crushed

2 tablespoons chopped fresh coriander

1–2 teaspoons chopped fresh chilli

1 egg

¾ teaspoon salt

2 tablespoons (30 g/1 oz) self-raising flour

oil for shallow frying

sweet chilli dipping sauce (page 243)

Drain corn if using canned, or thaw if using frozen. Place half the corn kernels in a food processor along with the garlic, coriander and chilli. Pulse briefly, then add the egg and salt, and chop again until corn is lightly crushed. Add remaining corn and flour, and pulse until well mixed but with some whole kernels remaining.

Heat 2.5 cm (1 in) oil in a large frying pan and fry spoonfuls of the batter until golden-brown, turning once or twice. Serve with sweet chilli sauce for dipping, and a small salad if desired.

Little Fish & Coconut Terrines

Makes 8–12

400 ml (13½ fl oz) coconut
    cream

2 teaspoons rice flour

salt

1 clove garlic, peeled

2 slices fresh ginger

1 teaspoon grated kaffir lime
    or lemon zest (optional)

1 fresh hot red chilli, deseeded
    and finely shredded

450 g (1 lb) firm white fish,
    cut into small cubes

1 egg

5 basil leaves, finely chopped

1 sprig fresh coriander or
    1 spring onion, for garnish

Brush 8–12 heatproof cups (e.g. 90-ml/3-fl oz Chinese tea cups) with oil.

Pour ¾ cup of the coconut cream into a small saucepan, add the rice flour and a small pinch of salt and simmer, stirring occasionally, until thickened.

Place the garlic, ginger, lime or lemon zest, and half the chilli in a food processor and grind to a smooth paste. Add the fish, egg and half the remaining coconut cream and blend until smooth. Stir in the remaining coconut cream, the basil and a few pinches of salt.

Three-quarters fill the prepared cups with the fish mixture, then spoon some of the coconut sauce over. Garnish with a coriander leaf or a few slices of spring onion, and some of the remaining chilli. Place cups in a steamer and steam for about 6 minutes, until firm.

Fish Cakes

Serves 4

350 g (12 oz) white or pink fish fillets, cut into small cubes

1 egg white

1–2 teaspoons red curry paste (page 234)

2 tablespoons (40 ml/1½ fl oz) fish sauce

2 green beans, very thinly sliced

4 kaffir lime leaves, finely shredded

oil for deep-frying

cucumber relish (page 239)

Place fish in a food processor with the egg white, curry paste and fish sauce. Process until well mixed, then add 2 tablespoons (40 ml/1½ fl oz) water and process again until mixture is sticky and soft. Tip into a bowl and mix in the beans and shredded lime leaves.

Heat oil to 180°C (360°F) in a wok or large pan.

With wet hands, form the fish mixture into cakes about 5 cm (2 in) in diameter and 5 mm (¼ in) thick. Slide cakes into the oil and fry, turning several times, until golden-brown all over. Drain briefly on paper towels, then serve immediately with cucumber relish for dipping.

ੴ These fish cakes should not be cooked in advance as they become tough.

Pork Balls

Serves 4–6

3 cloves garlic, peeled

2 fresh coriander roots

450 g (1 lb) finely minced pork

1 tablespoon (20 ml/¾ fl oz) fish sauce

1 teaspoon salt

ground white or black pepper

oil for frying

cubed fresh pineapple or melon (optional)

cucumber relish (page 239), for dipping

Place garlic and coriander roots in a food processor and grind to a paste. Add half the pork, the fish sauce, salt and a big pinch of pepper and process until well mixed. Tip into a bowl, add remaining pork and knead until soft and sticky. Use lightly oiled hands to form the mixture into walnut-sized balls.

Heat oil for shallow-frying or deep-frying, as preferred. Fry the meatballs, turning frequently, until they are golden-brown and cooked through (about 4 minutes).

Serve on toothpicks with little cubes of pineapple or melon (if using), and with cucumber relish on the side for dipping.

Pork Satay

2 teaspoons coriander seeds

1 teaspoon cumin seeds

⅓ teaspoon shrimp paste

4-cm (1½-in) piece fresh
lemongrass, chopped

1-cm (⅜-in) piece fresh ginger,
chopped

1 teaspoon salt

⅓ teaspoon ground turmeric

⅔ cup (160 ml/5½ fl oz)
coconut milk

450 g (1 lb) lean pork, cut into
2-cm (¾-in) strips

bamboo skewers, soaked for
30 minutes

satay sauce (page 241)

cucumber relish (page 239)

In a small frying pan dry-roast the coriander and cumin seeds and shrimp paste until fragrant, then transfer to a spice grinder and add lemongrass, ginger, salt and turmeric. Grind as finely as possible, then mix with the coconut milk. Pour mixture into a bowl with the pork, stir to combine, then leave to marinate for about 1 hour.

Thread the meat onto bamboo skewers (reserving the marinade). Heat a grill or charcoal barbecue to medium.

Cook the skewers, turning and brushing them with any remaining marinade, until well cooked and flecked dark-brown at the edges. Serve at once, with the dipping sauces offered in shallow dishes.

Coconut Prawns

Serves 4–6

12–18 raw (green) prawns, butterflied

salt and freshly ground black pepper

¾ cup (110 g/4 oz) plain flour

1 egg yolk

¾ cup iced water

1 cup shredded coconut

oil for deep-frying

chilli, garlic and vinegar dipping sauce (page 133) or sweet chilli dipping sauce (page 243)

Lightly season the prawns with salt and pepper, and coat very lightly with flour, shaking off excess.

Sift remaining flour into a bowl. Mix egg yolk with iced water and gradually pour into the flour, stirring gently, adding just enough liquid to form a thin, creamy batter (do not over-work). If batter is too thick, add a little more iced water.

Drag the prawns through the batter, then coat with shredded coconut.

Heat oil to 160°C (320°F) in a wok or large pan suitable for deep-frying.

Carefully slide the coconut-coated prawns into the oil and fry until golden-brown (about 1½ minutes). Remove, and drain briefly on paper towels. Serve immediately with your choice of dipping sauce.

Grilled Pork with Dipping Sauces

Serves 4–6

1½ teaspoons crushed garlic

½ teaspoon cracked white pepper

450 g (1 lb) pork tenderloin, trimmed of fat and skin

2 tablespoons freshly chopped coriander

chilli–lime dressing (page 244)

cucumber relish (page 239)

CARAMEL SAUCE

½ cup (110 g/4 oz) caster sugar

⅓ cup (80 ml/3 fl oz) fish sauce

To make the caramel sauce, melt sugar in a small saucepan and cook until dark-brown. Quickly remove from the heat and pour in fish sauce (the sugar may harden). Add 2–3 tablespoons (40–60 ml/1⅓–2 fl oz) water, return pan to heat and stir to dissolve. Simmer for 2 minutes, then set aside to cool.

Heat a charcoal barbecue or grill pan to medium–high.

Combine the garlic, pepper and 2 tablespoons caramel sauce. Brush evenly over the pork. Cook pork for about 12 minutes, turning frequently and occasionally brushing with oil to prevent sticking. (Alternatively, the pork can be browned in a pan, then cooked in a 200°C (390°F) oven for about 20 minutes.) Remove from the heat, cover with foil and set aside to rest for 5 minutes.

Stir coriander into the dressing. Slice pork thinly and arrange on a platter, with the dressing and relish offered in shallow dishes for dipping.

Stuffed Chicken Wings

Serves 6

1 piece black cloud ear (wood ear) fungus or 3–4 dried shiitake mushrooms

30 g (1 oz) bean-thread vermicelli

6 chicken wings

250 g (9 oz) pork mince

2 tablespoons finely chopped fresh coriander

2 tablespoons finely chopped water chestnuts

2 eggs

2 teaspoons fish sauce

⅓ cup (50 g/1¾ oz) cornflour or plain flour

1 cup fine dry breadcrumbs

oil for deep-frying

Soak fungus or mushrooms in boiling water for about 25 minutes. Soak bean-thread vermicelli in boiling water for 10 minutes, to soften.

Use a small sharp knife to cut carefully along the bones of each chicken wing, then push the meat away from the bones and twist the bones out, leaving only the bones in the very tip of each wing. (You can ask your butcher to do this for you.)

Place pork mince in a bowl with the coriander and water chestnuts, 1 egg yolk and the fish sauce. Mix thoroughly. Drain the vermicelli and fungus or mushrooms, and chop finely. Mix with the pork.

Carefully fill the deboned chicken wings with the pork mixture, without over-stuffing. Secure openings with toothpicks.

Beat remaining whole egg and egg white in a shallow dish. Put cornflour or flour in another shallow dish and the breadcrumbs in a third. Coat the wings in flour, then dip into beaten egg and finally coat evenly with breadcrumbs.

Heat oil to 170°C (340°F) in a wok or a large pan suitable for deep-frying.

Deep-fry the wings for 4–5 minutes, until golden-brown and cooked through. Carefully remove from the oil and drain on paper towels. Serve at once.

Curry Puffs

1 tablespoon (20 ml/¾ fl oz) oil

180 g (6½ oz) pork, chicken or beef mince

1 small onion, very finely chopped

1 clove garlic, crushed

2–3 teaspoons massaman curry paste

2 tablespoons chopped fresh coriander leaves

2 tablespoons chopped water chestnuts

salt or fish sauce, to taste

freshly ground black pepper

4–6 large square spring-roll wrappers

oil for deep-frying

Heat 1 tablespoon oil in wok and stir-fry the meat with the onion and garlic for 2 minutes. Add curry paste and cook for another 2 minutes, then add 3 tablespoons (60 ml/2 fl oz) water, the coriander and water chestnuts. Simmer, stirring occasionally, until liquid evaporates. Season to taste with salt or fish sauce, and the pepper, and set aside to cool.

Cut each wrapper into three strips. Place about 2½ teaspoons of filling on a corner of one strip and fold to make a triangle. Continue to fold in this way, to form a triangular pastry. Moisten the last fold with water, and press down.

Heat oil to 160°C (320°F) in a wok or a deep pan suitable for deep-frying. Fry the curry puffs until golden-brown (about 1½ minutes).

Stir-fried Minced Prawn on Sticky Rice

Serves 6

1½ cups cooked sticky rice (page 11)

250 g (9 oz) raw prawn meat

2 teaspoons fish sauce

1 sprig coriander, including root

1 clove garlic, peeled

1 spring onion (white part only), chopped

2 teaspoons peanut oil

salt and ground black pepper

freshly squeezed lime or lemon juice

2–3 teaspoons finely chopped fresh coriander

⅓ teaspoon finely chopped fresh hot red chilli

1 kaffir lime leaf, very finely shredded

lime or lemon wedges, to serve

Place a large piece of cling wrap on your work surface and brush with oil. Press the rice into a layer about 2 cm (¾ in) thick. Use an oiled 4-cm (1½-in) biscuit cutter to cut out six rounds of rice. Transfer to individual plates.

Blend the prawn meat, fish sauce, coriander sprig, garlic and spring onion in a food processor until slightly grainy. Heat oil in a small pan and stir-fry the prawn mixture until cooked and slightly sticky (about 1½ minutes). Season to taste with pepper, and salt or extra fish sauce. Add a squeeze of lime or lemon juice, and half the chopped coriander, chilli and lime leaf. Mix well. Top each rice cake with a spoonful of the prawn mixture and garnish with the remaining herbs, chilli and lime or lemon wedges.

Son-in-law Eggs

Serves 4–6

6 hard-boiled eggs

oil for deep-frying

1 medium-sized onion, thinly sliced

1 large fresh hot red chilli, thinly sliced

2 tablespoons (30 g/1½ oz) palm sugar or soft brown sugar

3½ tablespoons (70 ml/2½ fl oz) fish sauce

Peel the eggs and pat dry with paper towel.

Heat oil to about 160°C (320°F) in a wok or large pan suitable for deep-frying. Fry the eggs until the surface is well browned and blistering. Carefully lift out and drain on paper towels.

Fry the onion and half the chilli in the oil until crisp. Remove with a slotted spoon and set aside to drain.

Pour off all but 2 tablespoons of the oil, then reheat the pan, add the sugar and cook, without stirring, until golden-brown and caramelised. Remove from the heat, add the fish sauce and remaining chilli, and stir to combine. Return to the heat and simmer until slightly thickened.

Cut eggs in half and place yolk-side up on plates. Spoon on the sauce and garnish with the fried chilli and onion. Serve at once.

Spicy Grilled Quail

Serves 6

1½ tablespoons (30 ml/1 fl oz) fish sauce

1½ teaspoons cracked black pepper

1 tablespoon finely chopped coriander stems and root

1 teaspoon sugar

1 tablespoon (20 ml/¾ fl oz) sesame oil

6 quail, each cut into 4 pieces

chopped fresh coriander leaves, for garnish

1 fresh hot red chilli, deseeded and finely shredded

FIVE-SPICE SALT

1½ tablespoons fine salt

1½ teaspoons five-spice powder

To make the five-spice salt, tip salt into a wok over medium heat and cook, shaking pan occasionally, for about 1½ minutes. Remove from heat, add the five-spice powder and mix well. Tip onto a plate and leave to cool completely.

In a bowl, combine fish sauce, pepper, coriander, sugar and sesame oil. Rub this seasoning all over the quail pieces, cover and refrigerate for 1 hour.

Heat a grill or barbecue to medium–high. Cook the quail, turning occasionally, for 3–4 minutes, until browned on the outside and tender-pink inside. Arrange on a platter and garnish with chopped coriander and shredded chilli. Serve the five-spice salt on the side, for dipping.

Once cold, five-spice salt can be stored in a small jar for many months.

Steamed Egg with Pork & Prawns

Serves 4–6

3 large eggs

1 cup (250 ml/8½ fl oz) chicken stock or water

1 spring onion (white part and half the greens), finely chopped

1½ tablespoons (30 ml/1 fl oz) fish sauce

salt and freshly ground black pepper

150 g (5 oz) raw prawn meat, finely chopped

150 g (5 oz) pork mince

1 kaffir lime leaf, finely shredded

½ fresh hot red chilli, finely shredded

Beat the eggs into the chicken stock or water. Stir in the spring onion, fish sauce and a pinch each of salt and pepper. Add the prawn meat and pork mince and mix well.

Brush four or six small (approximately 180-ml/6-fl oz) heatproof dishes with oil, then fill with the egg mixture. Set the dishes in a steamer and steam for 12–15 minutes, until mixture is firm and cooked.

Serve immediately (in the dishes), garnished with shredded lime leaf and red chilli.

Fried Prawn Toasts

Serves 6

150 g (5 oz) raw prawn meat

30 g (1 oz) pork or bacon fat, finely diced

1 clove garlic, peeled

2 teaspoons fish sauce or light soy sauce

salt and freshly ground black pepper

1 large egg, separated

6 large slices square white bread

1 fresh mild red chilli, deseeded and very finely shredded

fresh coriander leaves, for garnish

oil for deep-frying

cucumber relish (page 239), to serve

Place prawn meat, pork or bacon fat, garlic and fish or soy sauce in a food processor and grind to a smooth paste. Add a pinch each of salt and pepper with the egg yolk and mix again. Spread mixture evenly over the bread.

Beat the egg white until slightly frothy and brush over the prawn topping, covering right to the edges. With a serrated knife, trim off the bread crusts and cut each slice into four squares or triangles. Press a shred of chilli and a coriander leaf onto each piece.

Heat oil to 180°C (360°F) and fry the bread, filled-side down, until golden-brown. Drain well on paper towels. Serve with cucumber relish on the side.

ौ The prawn meat can be substituted with minced pork, fish or chicken.

Soups & Salads

Thais enjoy soup at any time of the day – as a snack, a starter or a main course. It is even served for breakfast, in the form of a thin rice soup (*joek*). Thai soups fit into two main categories: tangy clear soups like the famous *tom yum gung* (a hot and sour prawn soup); and rich, creamy coconut soups like *tom kha kai* (which combines chicken and galangal in a mildly spiced liquid).

Crisp and crunchy or silky and sweet – almost anything goes when it comes to Thai salads. Roast meats, exotic mushrooms, tropical fruits, crisp noodles, succulent seafood, eggplant and tofu come together in interesting marriages with fresh, vibrant seasonings. Roasted peanuts, toasted coconut, fried dried shrimp, and deep-fried garlic and onion provide textural garnishes. Mixed salads make great first courses or lunch dishes, while a simple salad of green papaya is the perfect side dish for a curry or grill.

< Hot & Sour Prawn Soup (page 50)

Hot & Sour Prawn Soup

Tom yum gung

Serves 4

- 1 L (34 fl oz) fish stock or water
- 1 stem lemongrass, cut into 4 pieces
- 2 medium-sized fresh hot red chillies, deseeded
- 4 kaffir lime leaves
- ½ teaspoon chilli paste, or to taste
- 12–16 raw (green) prawns, butterflied
- 4 cherry tomatoes, cut in half
- 2 spring onions (white parts only), sliced
- 1½ tablespoons (30 ml/1 fl oz) fish sauce
- 2 tablespoons (40 ml/1½ fl oz) freshly squeezed lime or lemon juice, or to taste
- sugar, to taste
- fresh coriander, for garnish

Pour the stock or water into a saucepan and add lemongrass, chillies, lime leaves and chilli paste. Bring to the boil, then reduce heat and simmer for 5 minutes. Add prawns, tomatoes and spring onions, and simmer for 3 minutes. Season to taste with fish sauce, lime or lemon juice and a few pinches of sugar, to achieve a flavour that is hot and tangy.

Divide prawns, lemongrass, chillies, lime leaves and tomatoes evenly between four bowls, then ladle in broth and garnish with coriander leaves.

Chicken, Coconut & Galangal Soup

Serves 4–6

1 stem lemongrass, cut into 4 pieces

2-cm (¾-in) piece galangal or ginger, sliced

2 spring onions (white parts only), sliced

4 kaffir lime leaves (optional)

400 ml (13½ fl oz) coconut cream

180 g (6½ oz) chicken breast, diced

2 tablespoons (40 ml/1½ fl oz) fish sauce

12 canned straw mushrooms, cut in half

salt

1½ tablespoons (30 ml/1 fl oz) freshly squeezed lime or lemon juice

1 tablespoon chopped fresh coriander leaves or spring onion greens

Pour 2 cups (500 ml/17 fl oz) water into a saucepan and add lemongrass, galangal, spring onions and lime leaves (if using). Bring to the boil, then reduce heat and simmer for 2–3 minutes. Add coconut cream, chicken and fish sauce. Bring slowly back to the boil, then reduce heat to medium–low and simmer gently for 3 minutes. Add mushrooms and season to taste with salt and lime or lemon juice.

Discard lemongrass, galangal and lime leaves, then serve soup into bowls, evenly distributing the chicken and mushrooms. Garnish with coriander or spring onion greens.

Tamarind & Ginger Pork-rib Soup

Serves 4–6

2 cloves garlic, peeled

¾ teaspoon cracked black pepper

1 teaspoon salt

½ teaspoon shrimp paste (optional)

1 tablespoon (20 ml/¾ fl oz) oil

400 g (14 oz) pork spare ribs, chopped into short pieces

2-cm (¾-in) piece fresh ginger, cut into 4 slices

2 spring onions, cut into 4-cm (1½-in) pieces (whites and greens kept separate)

1½ tablespoons tamarind paste

2 small tomatoes, quartered

2 tablespoons (40 ml/1½ fl oz) fish sauce

sugar, to taste

Crush garlic with pepper, salt and shrimp paste in a mortar.

Heat the oil in a heavy-based saucepan and fry the garlic paste for 1 minute. Add 1.5 L (3 pt 3 fl oz) water to the pan, along with the pork ribs, ginger and the white parts of the spring onions. Bring to the boil, then reduce heat and simmer for about 30 minutes, or until pork is almost tender.

Add tamarind paste, tomatoes and fish sauce to the pan. Taste, and adjust seasoning with a pinch or two of sugar. Simmer a further 5–10 minutes, then stir in the spring-onion greens. Divide evenly between soup bowls.

Meatball & Basil Soup

Serves 4–6

250 g (9 oz) lean beef, diced

2 tablespoons (40 ml/1½ fl oz) fish sauce

1 clove garlic, crushed

⅓ teaspoon freshly ground black pepper

1 L (34 fl oz) chicken stock

3–4 small bird's eye chillies

2 spring onions, sliced

18 fresh basil leaves (preferably Thai holy basil)

Place beef in a food processor with 2 teaspoons of the fish sauce, plus the garlic and pepper, and grind to a smooth paste. Transfer to a bowl.

Heat the stock in a large pan and add the chillies and spring onions (reserve some of the green parts for garnish).

With wet hands, shape the beef into bite-size balls. Slide balls gently into the soup and simmer for about 6 minutes, until cooked through.

Remove soup from the heat and stir in the basil. Divide evenly into bowls and garnish with reserved spring onion greens.

Mushroom Soup

Serves 4–6

220 g (8 oz) Asian mushrooms (shiitake, oyster, giant oyster, enoki)

225 g (8 oz) canned straw mushrooms, drained

5 thin slices fresh ginger

1 tablespoon (20 ml/¾ fl oz) fish sauce or light soy sauce

1.25 L (2 pt 10 fl oz) chicken or vegetable stock

2 tablespoons (30 g/1 oz) cornflour

salt and freshly ground black pepper

Cut large mushrooms into strips and cut straw mushrooms in half.

Place all of the ingredients (except cornflour) in a saucepan and bring to the boil. Simmer for 5–6 minutes. Mix cornflour with 2 tablespoons (40 ml/1½ fl oz) cold water and stir into the soup. Simmer until it thickens. Check seasoning, adding salt and pepper to taste.

Mushroom-flavoured stock cubes make an excellent base for this soup.

Seafood Soup

Serves 4–6

1.25 L (2 pt 10 fl oz) fish stock or water

1 stem lemongrass, cut into 3–4 pieces

⅓ teaspoon fennel seeds, lightly crushed

450 g (1 lb) mixed raw seafood (shelled prawns, squid rings or squares, fish cubes, mussels)

3 kaffir lime leaves, torn in half

1 strip lime, lemon or orange zest

6 small fresh green bird's eye chillies (optional)

1 large fresh hot red chilli, deseeded and sliced

fish sauce, fresh lime juice and sugar to taste

Bring the stock or water to the boil in a large saucepan, then add lemongrass and fennel seeds. Reduce heat and simmer for 5 minutes. Add all the seafood, along with the lime leaves, zest and chillies. Simmer just long enough to cook the seafood (3–4 minutes).

Taste and add fish sauce, lime juice and sugar, to achieve a flavour that is slightly tart and pleasantly salty.

If you buy unshelled prawns, you can use the shells to make the stock.

Hot & Tangy Cabbage, Bean Sprout & Coconut Soup

Serves 4–6

150 g (5 oz) Chinese cabbage, roughly chopped

150 g (5 oz) fresh bean sprouts

3 shallots or 1 small onion, peeled

2 fresh hot red chillies, deseeded

2 cloves garlic, peeled

1 L (34 fl oz) coconut milk

1 stem lemongrass, cut in half

2 slices galangal or ginger

2 kaffir lime leaves, torn in half (optional)

2½ tablespoons (50 ml/ 1¾ fl oz) freshly squeezed lime juice

2½ tablespoons (50 ml/ 1¾ fl oz) fish sauce

Blanch cabbage and bean sprouts in boiling water and drain. Set aside.

Place shallots or onion, red chillies and garlic in a spice grinder and grind to a paste.

Heat ½ cup (125 ml/4 fl oz) of the coconut milk in a saucepan or wok and add the onion paste. Simmer for 3 minutes, stirring.

Add remaining coconut milk to the soup, along with lemongrass, galangal or ginger, and kaffir lime leaves. Bring to the boil, then reduce heat and simmer for 2–3 minutes, stirring often.

Add cabbage and bean sprouts to the soup, along with ½–1 cup (125–250 ml/4–8 fl oz) water if needed. Simmer for about 6 minutes, stirring occasionally, until cabbage is tender. Season to taste with the lime juice and fish sauce, to achieve a tangy, spicy flavour.

Rice Congee

Joek

Serves 4–6

2¼ cups jasmine rice

2 teaspoons sliced garlic

oil for frying

3 cups (750 ml/25 fl oz) chicken stock

salt and ground white pepper

150 g (5 oz) sliced cooked meat (pork, duck, beef) or raw chicken

¼ cup chopped spring onion greens

1½ tablespoons crushed roasted peanuts

3–4 tablespoons shredded salted radish or cabbage

1–2 teaspoons chopped fresh red chilli

Place rice in a large saucepan and add 2 L (4 pt 4 fl oz) water. Bring to the boil, then reduce heat and simmer for about 1 hour, stirring occasionally.

Meanwhile, fry the garlic in a little oil until crisp.

Add chicken stock to the pot with the rice, with salt and pepper to taste. Continue to simmer for a further 20 minutes, until the rice is breaking up. Add the raw chicken (if using), and cook for 2 minutes.

Serve into bowls and scatter cooked meat and remaining ingredients over.

Tofu Soup with Baby Corn, Mushrooms & Choko

Serves 4–6

225 g (8 oz) soft tofu, cut into small cubes

1 L (34 fl oz) vegetable or mushroom stock

1 spring onion, thinly sliced (whites and greens kept separate)

½ choko (or use zucchini), diced

225 g (8 oz) canned or fresh baby corn

225 g (8 oz) canned straw mushrooms (or 75 g/2½ oz) oyster mushrooms), cut in half

1–2 tablespoons light soy sauce or fish sauce

salt and sugar, to taste

Divide tofu between the soup bowls.

In a saucepan, bring stock to the boil and add white parts of spring onion, with the choko and baby corn. Simmer for 3 minutes. Add mushrooms to the soup and simmer for 1–2 minutes. Season to taste with soy or fish sauce, salt and a large pinch of sugar, and simmer briefly.

Ladle soup over the tofu and garnish with reserved spring-onion greens.

Mushroom-flavoured stock cubes make an excellent mushroom stock.

Grilled Beef & Bean-thread Noodle Salad

Serves 3–4

90 g (3 oz) bean-thread vermicelli

2 teaspoons red curry paste (page 234)

300 g (10½ oz) beef rump or sirloin steak

1 medium-sized red onion, thinly sliced

1 small cucumber, sliced

½ red capsicum, cut into matchsticks

1½ cups mixed fresh herbs (coriander, basil, mint)

1–2 tablespoons chopped roasted peanuts, for garnish

DRESSING

2 tablespoons (40 ml/1½ fl oz) freshly squeezed lime juice

2 teaspoons sugar

1 tablespoon (20 ml/¾ fl oz) fish sauce

Soak vermicelli in hot water for 10 minutes, to soften.

Rub the curry paste into the steak and set aside for 10 minutes. Meanwhile, heat a barbecue or heavy grill pan to high. Brush steak lightly with oil and grill for about 3 minutes on each side. Remove, cover, and let rest for 4–5 minutes.

Drain vermicelli and cut into short lengths. Combine in a salad bowl with onion, cucumber, capsicum and herbs.

To make the dressing, whisk lime juice, sugar and fish sauce together. Pour two-thirds over the salad and toss well. Slice the steak and drape over the salad. Drizzle the remaining dressing over and scatter with peanuts.

Pork & Peanut Salad

1 tablespoon (20 ml/¾ fl oz) oil

350 g (12 oz) pork mince (or use chicken)

juice of 2 limes

about 2½ tablespoons (50 ml/1¾ fl oz) fish sauce

1 tablespoon (15 g/¾ oz) palm sugar or soft brown sugar

4 sprigs fresh coriander, chopped

4 sprigs fresh mint, leaves torn

2 spring onions, chopped

2 tablespoons roasted peanuts, coarsely ground

lettuce leaves, to serve

1 small red onion, sliced into thin rings, for garnish

1 fresh hot red chilli, deseeded and finely shredded, for garnish

Heat oil in a frying pan or wok, then add mince and cook for a few minutes, stirring, until barely cooked. Drain off any liquid and tip meat into a bowl. Add the lime juice, fish sauce, sugar, herbs, spring onions and half the ground peanuts. Mix well.

Serve salad on lettuce leaves, garnished with the onion rings, chilli and remaining peanuts.

Chicken Salad with Mint & Coriander

Serves 3–4

250 g (9 oz) chicken breast fillet, skin off

1 spring onion, finely chopped

⅔ cup fresh mint leaves, roughly chopped

½ cup fresh coriander leaves, roughly chopped

1½ teaspoons caster sugar

½ teaspoon dried chilli flakes, or to taste

about 2½ tablespoons (50 ml/1¾ fl oz) fish sauce

3½ tablespoons (70 ml/2 fl oz) freshly squeezed lime juice

Place the chicken in a steamer and steam for about 6 minutes, until cooked. Remove and allow to cool. Chop roughly, then place in a food processor and chop finely. Transfer to a salad bowl and add spring onion and half the herbs.

Place remaining herbs in the food processor, along with the sugar and chilli flakes. Chop for just a few seconds. Add fish sauce and lime juice, and pulse briefly to combine, then taste and adjust seasonings. Pour herb dressing over the salad and mix thoroughly. Cover and chill for 20 minutes before serving.

Green Papaya Salad

Som tam

Serves 4–6

3 cups grated green (unripe) papaya (or mango)

¾ cup grated carrot, unripe pear or green apple

1 small onion, finely diced

3 tablespoons chopped fresh coriander leaves

DRESSING

2½ tablespoons (50 ml/1¾ fl oz) freshly squeezed lime juice

3 tablespoons (60 ml/2 fl oz) fish sauce

1 tablespoon (15 g/¾ oz) palm sugar or soft brown sugar, or to taste

½ teaspoon dried chilli flakes, or to taste

Combine grated ingredients in a bowl with onion and herbs.

In another small bowl whisk together the dressing ingredients. Taste and adjust seasonings, adding a little more lime juice, fish sauce or sugar as needed, to give a tangy, slightly sweet dressing.

Pour dressing over the salad and toss well. Cover and refrigerate for 20 minutes before serving.

Peeled and sliced green mango is sold in many Asian food stores.

Spicy Chicken Salad

Serves 6

1 roasted, barbecued or char-grilled chicken maryland (page 136)

chilli–lime dressing (page 244)

1 small head curly endive, leaves separated

6 cherry tomatoes, cut in half

2 small red onions, sliced into thin rings

1–2 tablespoons chopped roasted peanuts

4 hard-boiled eggs, cut into wedges (optional)

6 spring onions, cut into curls

Remove chicken meat from the bone, leaving skin on. Tear into small strips and place in a bowl. Add about 3 tablespoons (60 ml/2 fl oz) of the dressing and toss lightly to coat.

Arrange the endive, tomatoes and red onion on a serving platter and scatter the chicken over the top. Sprinkle the peanuts over and surround with wedges of egg (if using). Garnish with the spring onions.

- You could make this salad with spicy grilled quail (page 44).

- To make the spring-onion curls, cut an 8-cm (3-in) piece from the base of each spring onion. Trim off the roots, and at the other end use the point of a sharp knife to make several slits down the spring onion, cutting almost to the base. When placed in iced water the feathered sections will curl up.

Calamari & Bean Sprout Salad

Serves 4–6

6 small fresh squid, cleaned

150 g (5 oz) fresh bean sprouts

2 medium-sized red onions, sliced

2.5-cm (1-in) piece fresh young ginger, very finely shredded

2 sticks celery, thinly sliced at an angle

2–3 sprigs fresh coriander, chopped

2–3 sprigs fresh mint, leaves torn

2 sprigs fresh basil, leaves torn

1–2 fresh hot red chillies, deseeded and finely shredded

chilli–lime dressing (page 244)

4 lettuce leaves, shredded

Rinse and drain the squid and cut into thin rings. Cover with boiling water and let sit for 20 seconds, then drain.

Blanch the bean sprouts, onions and ginger in boiling water, then drain and refresh in ice-cold water. Drain.

In a salad bowl, combine the squid, bean sprouts, onions, ginger and celery with the herbs and chillies. Add 3–4 tablespoons of the chilli-lime dressing and toss lightly.

Serve the salad piled over shredded lettuce. Spoon on a little more dressing just before serving.

Noodle Salad with Chicken, Prawns & Roast Pork

Serves 4–6

90 g (3 oz) bean-thread vermicelli

2 tablespoons dried shrimp

2 cloves garlic, sliced (optional)

2 tablespoons (40 ml/1½ fl oz) oil

100 g (3½ oz) chicken breast, finely shredded

12 small raw (green) prawns, shelled and deveined

120 g (4 oz) roast pork or Chinese *cha siu* pork, shredded

1 red onion, thinly sliced

1 stick celery, thinly sliced

½ red capsicum, thinly sliced

1 small curly-leaf lettuce or 4 Chinese cabbage leaves

CORIANDER & CHILLI DRESSING

2 tablespoons (40 ml/1½ fl oz) rice vinegar

1 tablespoon (15 g/¾ oz) palm sugar, or more to taste

2 tablespoons (40 ml/1½ fl oz) sweet chilli sauce

4 sprigs fresh coriander, chopped

Soak vermicelli in hot water for 10 minutes, to soften. Combine dressing ingredients with a few teaspoons water.

Fry the dried shrimp and garlic in the oil until crisp, then remove to a plate using a slotted spoon. Sauté the chicken and prawns in the same oil until lightly cooked (about 1½ minutes). Tip onto a plate to cool.

In a bowl, combine drained, chopped noodles with pork, chicken, prawns, onion, celery and capsicum. Arrange salad over lettuce leaves, pour the dressing over and garnish with the fried shrimp and garlic.

Prawn & Kaffir Lime Salad

Serves 4

12 large green (raw) prawns, in their shells

2 tablespoons (40 ml/1½ fl oz) fish sauce

1½ tablespoons (30 ml/1 fl oz) freshly squeezed lime juice

1 stem lemongrass, cut into paper-thin slices

4 shallots or 1 medium-sized red onion, thinly sliced

5–6 sprigs fresh mint, leaves shredded

5–6 sprigs fresh coriander, chopped

2–3 fresh hot red chillies, deseeded and finely shredded

1-cm (⅜-in) piece fresh ginger, finely shredded

3 kaffir lime leaves, very finely shredded

Boil the prawns in salted water for 4–6 minutes, then drain, shell and cut in half lengthways. Place in a bowl with the fish sauce and lime juice, and leave to cool.

Combine lemongrass, shallots, herbs, chilli, ginger and lime leaves. Add the prawns and their marinade, and mix well. Serve salad on small plates or in bowls.

Pomelo Salad

Serves 4

1 pomelo (or 2 grapefruit, preferably pink)

1½ tablespoons (30 ml/1 fl oz) fish sauce

3–4 teaspoons palm sugar

2 teaspoons freshly squeezed lime juice

½ teaspoon crushed chilli

150 g (5 oz) small cooked and shelled prawns

1 medium-sized red onion, thinly sliced

1 fresh hot red chilli, deseeded and finely shredded

1 fresh hot green chilli, deseeded and finely shredded

3 tablespoons chopped fresh coriander and mint (or basil)

2 tablespoons toasted shredded coconut

Working over a bowl to catch the juices, peel the pomelo (or grapefruit), separate flesh into segments and cut each segment into three or four pieces.

To the juices in the bowl, add the fish sauce, sugar, lime juice and crushed chilli, and mix well. Taste and adjust seasonings as needed. Add pomelo pieces, prawns, onion, shredded chillies and herbs, and mix well. Transfer to a serving plate and garnish with toasted coconut.

To toast coconut, heat a small non-stick pan over medium heat. Add coconut and cook slowly, stirring with a wooden spoon, until golden-brown. Remove and let cool.

Roasted Eggplant Salad

Serves 4–6

4 slender oriental eggplant

1 medium-sized red onion, thinly sliced

1 tablespoon (20 ml/¾ fl oz) fish sauce

2 tablespoons (40 ml/1½ fl oz) freshly squeezed lime juice

2 teaspoons caster sugar

2 tablespoons chopped fresh coriander leaves

6 cherry tomatoes, cut in half

2–3 hard-boiled eggs, cut into 8 wedges

1 large lime, cut into wedges

1 small cucumber, sliced

crisp-fried onions (page 206), for garnish (optional)

chopped roasted peanuts, for garnish (optional)

Place the eggplant in a 220°C (420°F) oven (or hold directly over a gas flame, turning frequently), and cook until very tender and skin is blackened. Transfer to a bowl, cover with cling wrap and leave for 5 minutes (the trapped steam will loosen the skins). Peel, chop the flesh, then transfer to a bowl.

Add to the eggplant the red onion, fish sauce, lime juice, sugar and coriander. Adjust seasonings if necessary. Arrange on a platter with tomatoes, egg and lime wedges, and cucumber slices. Garnish with crisp-fried onions and/or peanuts.

Cucumber & Crisp-fried Tofu Salad with Peanut Dressing

Serves 4–5

oil for deep-frying

180 g (6½ oz) firm tofu, cut into bite-size pieces

2 small cucumbers, halved lengthways and thinly sliced

8 cherry tomatoes, cut in half

2 tablespoons chopped fresh coriander leaves

8–12 fresh mint or basil leaves, torn

1 tablespoon finely chopped roasted peanuts, for garnish

DRESSING

½ teaspoon chilli paste or crushed chilli

3 teaspoons freshly squeezed lemon juice

3 teaspoons palm sugar or soft brown sugar

salt

2 tablespoons chopped spring onion

2–3 tablespoons finely chopped roasted peanuts

Heat oil to 180°C (360°F) in a wok or a large pan suitable for deep-frying. Fry the tofu, turning constantly, until golden-brown. Remove and drain on paper towels.

Combine cucumbers, tomatoes, coriander, and mint or basil in a bowl.

To make the dressing, whisk chilli with lemon juice, sugar and ½ cup (125 ml/4 fl oz) water. Add salt to taste and stir in spring onion and peanuts.

Pour dressing over the salad, add tofu and toss lightly. Pile onto plates and garnish with chopped peanuts.

Curries

Thai curries are aromatic, luscious and bright. A number of colourful curry pastes are used, with varying flavours and degrees of heat. Red pastes, made with red chillies, are hot; they suit meats like pork, duck and beef, and also go well with shellfish. Green pastes contain green chillies and fresh herbs, and are very hot; they go well with fish and shellfish, chicken and vegetables. Yellow pastes are made from turmeric root and orange–red chillies and are of medium heat; they marry well with seafood and vegetables, but can also be used with beef, lamb and chicken. Massaman curry pastes feature Indian spices, while Panang-style pastes are of Malaysian origin; both are mild to medium.

All of these curry pastes are now readily available, but making your own is rewarding (see recipes in Extras). Note that purchased curry pastes are generally hotter than homemade ones. Serve Thai curries with steamed jasmine rice, and cucumber or tomato on the side to balance the heat.

‹ Red Beef Curry (page 80)

Red Beef Curry

Serves 4

1 small carrot, thinly sliced

8–10 green beans or 1 small zucchini, sliced

400 ml (13½ fl oz) coconut cream

1 tablespoon red curry paste (page 234)

1 small onion, thinly sliced

8 button mushrooms, quartered

½ red capsicum, diced

salt and freshly ground black pepper

fish sauce, to taste

300 g (10½ oz) very thinly sliced beef topside or rump

freshly squeezed lime or lemon juice (optional)

Parboil carrots and beans or zucchini in salted water for about 3½ minutes, until almost tender. Drain and set aside.

In another saucepan, simmer one-third of the coconut cream with the curry paste and onion for 3–4 minutes, stirring often. Add mushrooms and capsicum, and cook for another 2 minutes, stirring often. Stir in remaining coconut cream and ½ cup (125 ml/4 fl oz) water, bring to the boil, then reduce heat and simmer for 2 minutes. Season to taste with salt and pepper and add a generous splash of fish sauce. Add drained vegetables and the beef, and simmer just long enough for the beef to change colour. Finish with a few teaspoons of lime or lemon juice for a tangy flavour.

Panang Beef Curry

Serves 4–5

400 ml (13½ fl oz) coconut cream

2 tablespoons panang curry paste

1 fresh hot red chilli, deseeded and sliced (optional)

¾ cup (180 ml/6 fl oz) beef stock or water

500 g beef rump, cut into very thin strips

2 tablespoons (30 g/1½ oz) palm sugar or soft brown sugar

2 tablespoons (40 ml/1½ fl oz) fish sauce

3 tablespoons smooth or crunchy peanut butter

8–10 fresh basil leaves

Pour half the coconut cream into a wok or saucepan and add the curry paste and chilli. Simmer, stirring, for 3–4 minutes, until oil is released and floats on the surface. Pour in remaining coconut cream and stock or water, and bring to the boil. Add the beef strips, sugar and fish sauce, and simmer for 2–3 minutes, stirring occasionally.

Remove a ladleful of liquid from the pan and mix with the peanut butter until smooth, then pour back into the pan. Stir in basil leaves and simmer for 1–2 minutes. Check seasonings and serve.

Instead of a panang paste, you can use a yellow or massaman curry paste with extra peanuts added.

Massaman Beef Curry

Serves 4–6

3 tablespoons (60 ml/2 fl oz) oil

450 g (1 lb) braising beef, cut into small cubes

3 medium-sized potatoes, cut into cubes

5 cardamom pods

1 cinnamon stick

2½ cups (625 ml/21 fl oz) coconut cream

2–3 tablespoons roasted peanuts (optional)

2–3 tablespoons massaman curry paste

1 teaspoon palm sugar

2 tablespoons (40 ml/1½ fl oz) fish sauce

2–3 teaspoons tamarind paste

salt

Heat oil in a wok and brown the beef in two batches. Set aside. Add potatoes to the pan and brown, adding more oil if needed. Set aside. Return meat to the pan and add spices, half the coconut cream and 1 cup (250 ml/8½ fl oz) water. Bring to the boil, then reduce heat and simmer for about 30 minutes. Add potatoes and peanuts and simmer gently, stirring occasionally, until meat and potatoes are almost cooked (about 10 minutes).

In a small pan, heat the remaining coconut cream with the curry paste and cook for about 3 minutes, stirring. Add sugar, fish sauce and tamarind paste and simmer for 2–3 minutes. Pour mixture into the curry and check for salt. Simmer for about another 15 minutes, then taste and adjust with extra fish sauce, sugar or tamarind as necessary.

Pork Curry from the North-west

Serves 6

2 tablespoons (40 ml/1½ fl oz) oil

1 kg (2 lb 3 oz) pork shoulder or belly (skin on), cut into 4-cm (1½-in) cubes

1 medium-sized onion, diced

4 cloves garlic, crushed

2 tablespoons finely chopped lemongrass

3 teaspoons crushed fresh ginger

1½ teaspoons shrimp paste (optional)

1 teaspoon crushed red chilli, or to taste

1–1½ tablespoons yellow curry paste

2 teaspoons dark soy sauce

3 teaspoons tamarind paste

1 tablespoon (15 g/¾ oz) palm sugar or soft brown sugar, or to taste

salt or fish sauce, to taste

Heat oil in a wok or heavy-based saucepan over high heat and brown the pork with the onion, garlic and lemongrass (about 5 minutes). Add the ginger, shrimp paste, chilli and curry paste, and cook a further 2–3 minutes, over medium heat, stirring constantly.

Add soy sauce, tamarind and sugar to the curry, with enough water to barely cover the pork. Bring to the boil, then reduce to a simmer, partially cover and cook gently for about 35 minutes, until pork is tender. Taste for seasoning, adding salt or fish sauce if needed.

Pork Red Curry with Beans & Cabbage

Serves 4

2 cups shredded cabbage

90 g (3 oz) green beans, sliced

2 tablespoons (40 ml/1½ fl oz) oil

1½ tablespoons red curry paste (page 234)

300 g (10½ oz) pork tenderloin, thinly sliced

1½ tablespoons finely chopped lemongrass

2 tablespoons (40 ml/1½ fl oz) fish sauce

6 fresh shiitake or Swiss brown mushrooms, sliced

1–2 fresh hot red chillies, deseeded and sliced

salt and sugar, to taste

⅓ cup (80 ml/3 fl oz) coconut cream (optional)

fresh coriander, basil or mint leaves, for garnish

Parboil the cabbage and beans in lightly salted water until barely tender. Drain well.

Heat oil in a wok and stir-fry the curry paste, pork and lemongrass for 2 minutes. Add fish sauce, mushrooms, chillies and drained vegetables, and stir-fry until well mixed. Taste, and add salt and sugar as needed. Stir in coconut cream (if using) and gently heat through.

Serve garnished with plenty of the herbs.

Chicken & Bamboo Red Curry

Serves 4–6

1 cup (250 ml/8½ fl oz)
  coconut milk

4 teaspoons red curry paste
  (page 234)

450 g (1 lb) chicken thigh
  fillets, cut into 2-cm (¾-in)
  cubes

1 small onion, cut into wedges

120 g (4 oz) sliced bamboo
  shoots

3 kaffir lime leaves, torn in
  half (optional)

1½ teaspoons palm sugar or
  soft brown sugar

2 tablespoons (40 ml/1½ fl oz)
  fish sauce

4 cherry tomatoes, cut in half

salt

8–10 fresh basil leaves

Pour the coconut milk into a wok or saucepan and add curry paste. Simmer for 5 minutes, stirring occasionally. Add chicken and onion to the pan, stirring to coat with the sauce, and simmer for 5 minutes. Add bamboo shoots, lime leaves, sugar, fish sauce and ½ cup (125 ml/4 fl oz) water. Bring to the boil, stir in tomatoes and simmer for another 5 minutes, until chicken and tomatoes are tender. Check for salt. Stir in basil leaves just before serving.

Green Chicken Curry

Serves 4–5

1 small carrot, sliced

8 green beans or 2 snake beans, cut into pieces

400 ml (13½ fl oz) coconut cream

4 teaspoons green curry paste (page 235)

1 stem lemongrass, cut in half

400 g (14 oz) chicken breast fillet, cut into bite-size pieces

8 straw or oyster mushrooms, cut in half

60 g (2 oz) sliced bamboo shoots

4 cherry tomatoes, cut in half

2 spring onions, cut into 2.5-cm (1-in) pieces

2½ tablespoons (50 ml/ 1¾ fl oz) fish sauce

2–3 teaspoons sugar

freshly squeezed lime juice

lime wedges and fresh basil leaves, to serve

Parboil carrot and beans in lightly salted water for 3 minutes. Heat half the coconut cream in a wok with the curry paste and lemongrass, and simmer, stirring, for 2 minutes. Add remaining coconut cream and 2 cups (500 ml/ 17 fl oz) water and bring to the boil. Add chicken, cooked and raw vegetables (reserve some of the spring onion greens). Simmer for about 5 minutes, stirring occasionally.

Season curry to taste with fish sauce, sugar and lime. When chicken and vegetables are tender, stir in basil. Serve in bowls, garnished with spring-onion greens, and with lime wedges on the side.

Duck & Pumpkin Yellow Curry

Serves 3–5

4 shallots or spring onions, sliced

1 large fresh hot red chilli, deseeded and sliced

1 stem lemongrass, sliced

200 ml (7 fl oz) coconut cream

2½ tablespoons yellow curry paste

1 tablespoon (20 ml/¾ fl oz) fish sauce

2 teaspoons palm sugar

2 duck breast fillets (about 450 g/1 lb in total), skin on, cut into 1-cm slices

250 g (9 oz) pumpkin, cut into chunks

salt and freshly ground black pepper

chopped fresh coriander or basil leaves, to serve

Heat a wok and add shallots or spring onions, chilli, lemongrass, coconut cream and curry paste. Simmer, stirring, for 4 minutes. Add 1 cup (250 ml/ 8½ fl oz) water, the fish sauce and sugar, and bring to a simmer. Add the duck and cook gently for 10 minutes. Add pumpkin and continue to simmer until duck and pumpkin are tender (about 10 minutes).

Season to taste with salt and pepper, and stir in the herbs before serving.

Roast Duck Curry with Lychees

Serves 3–4

½ Chinese roast duck

4 teaspoons red curry paste (page 234)

400 ml (13½ fl oz) coconut cream

2 teaspoons ground sweet paprika

2 mild fresh red chillies, deseeded

2–3 kaffir lime leaves, torn in half

1 tablespoon (15 g/¾ oz) palm sugar or soft brown sugar

2 tablespoons (40 ml/1½ fl oz) fish sauce

8 fresh or canned lychees, cut in half

salt

freshly squeezed lime juice

fresh basil leaves, to serve (optional)

Remove duck breast and thigh meat, and slice. Chop the leg into pieces, cutting through the bone.

Heat curry paste with half the coconut cream in a wok or saucepan and simmer for about 2½ minutes, stirring occasionally. Add remaining coconut cream, ⅓ cup (80 ml/3 fl oz) water, paprika, chillies, lime leaves, sugar and fish sauce. Simmer for 3–4 minutes.

Add duck and lychees to the sauce and heat gently. Check seasoning, adding salt and a big squeeze of lime juice. Stir basil (if using) into the sauce, and serve.

Red Fish Curry

Serves 4-6

½ teaspoon ground turmeric

1½ tablespoons (30 ml/1 fl oz) oil

4 mackerel steaks (or use flathead fillets)

400 ml (13½ fl oz) coconut cream

2 tablespoons red curry paste (page 234)

½ cup (125 ml/4 fl oz) fish stock or water

2-3 kaffir lime leaves, torn in half

2½ tablespoons (50 ml/1¾ fl oz) fish sauce

1 tablespoon (15 g/¾ oz) palm sugar or soft brown sugar, or to taste

fresh coriander leaves, for garnish

Mix turmeric with the oil and brush over both sides of the mackerel. Heat a large frying pan and fry the fish until golden-brown (3-3½ minutes on each side). Set aside.

Pour one-third of the coconut cream into the same frying pan and stir in curry paste. Simmer, stirring, for 3-4 minutes, until oil is released and floats on the surface. Add remaining coconut cream, and fish stock or water. Bring to the boil, then reduce heat and simmer for 2-3 minutes. Gently slide the fish into the sauce and add the lime leaves. Simmer for about 2 minutes or until fish is cooked. Stir in fish sauce and palm sugar to taste, and serve garnished with the coriander.

Green Prawn Curry

1 snake bean or 4–6 green beans, sliced

1 small carrot, sliced

1–2 tablespoons green curry paste (page 235)

2 tablespoons (40 ml/1½ fl oz) oil

400 ml (13½ fl oz) coconut milk

4 kaffir lime leaves, torn in half

1 stem lemongrass, cut into 4–5 pieces

60 g (2 oz) sliced bamboo shoots

24 medium-sized green (raw) prawns, butterflied

1½ tablespoons (30 ml/ 1 fl oz) fish sauce

pinch of sugar

8–10 fresh basil leaves

Parboil beans and carrot in lightly salted water for about 3 minutes. Drain.

Fry curry paste in oil for 1 minute, then add a third of the coconut milk and cook for 2–3 minutes. Add lime leaves, lemongrass and 1 cup (250 ml/ 8½ fl oz) water and bring to the boil. Pour in remaining coconut milk, bring to the boil, then reduce to a simmer and cook for 2–3 minutes. Add beans, carrot, bamboo shoots, prawns, fish sauce and a large pinch of sugar and simmer gently for about 2 minutes, until prawns are just cooked. Check seasoning and adjust if necessary. Stir in the basil leaves and serve.

Yellow Prawn Curry

Serves 4

400 ml (13½ fl oz) coconut cream

1 tablespoon yellow curry paste

2 tablespoons (40 ml/1½ fl oz) fish sauce

1–2 teaspoons palm sugar

6 cherry tomatoes, cut in half

½ small cucumber, diced

2 kaffir lime leaves, torn in half (optional)

450 g (1 lb) peeled and deveined green (raw) prawns

salt

Pour half the coconut cream into a wok or saucepan and bring to the boil. Reduce heat and simmer for 5 minutes, then add the curry paste and simmer another 5 minutes, stirring occasionally. Add the fish sauce, sugar, remaining coconut milk and ¾ cup (180 ml/6 fl oz) water, and simmer for a further 6–7 minutes, stirring. Add tomatoes, cucumber and lime leaves, and simmer for 2–3 minutes. Add prawns and cook for about another 2 minutes, until pink and firm. Check seasonings, adding salt to taste.

Chu Chi Prawn Curry

1½ tablespoons dried shrimp

1 stem lemongrass, trimmed

½ teaspoon shrimp paste

1 tablespoon (20 ml/¾ fl oz) oil

3 teaspoons red curry paste (page 234)

½–1 teaspoon crushed red chilli

½ cup (125 ml/4 fl oz) coconut milk

12 green beans or 2–3 snake beans, cut into 4-cm (1½-in) lengths

1 tomato, cut into wedges

18–24 medium-sized green (raw) prawns, shelled and deveined but tails left on

1½ tablespoons (30 ml/1 fl oz) fish sauce

2 teaspoons caster sugar or palm sugar

salt

freshly squeezed lime or lemon juice

Bring ½ cup (125 ml/4 fl oz) water to the boil, pour over the dried shrimp and soak for 15–20 minutes. Finely slice 2.5 cm (1 in) of the lemongrass and put into a food processor or blender with the shrimp (and its soaking water) and shrimp paste. Grind to a reasonably smooth purée. >

Heat the oil in a wok or saucepan and fry the purée with the curry paste and chilli for a few seconds. Add coconut milk and simmer over high heat, stirring continuously, for about 3 minutes. Add 1½ cups (375 ml/12½ fl oz) water, along with the beans, tomato and remaining lemongrass. Simmer for 4 minutes.

Add the prawns, fish sauce and sugar to the curry and simmer until prawns are pink and firm (about 2 minutes). Check seasoning, adding salt and lime or lemon juice to taste. Remove lemongrass stem before serving.

இ *Chu chi* curries are named for the 'sputtering' sound of the curry paste frying in the pan.

Red Curry of Mushrooms & Zucchini

Serves 4–6

400 ml (13½ fl oz) coconut milk

3–5 teaspoons red curry paste (page 234)

1½ teaspoons palm sugar or soft brown sugar

2½ tablespoons (50 ml/ 1¾ fl oz) fish sauce

200 g (7 oz) mixed Asian mushrooms (straw, oyster, shiitake, enoki)

1 zucchini, sliced

3 spring onions, cut into 4-cm (1½-in) pieces

1 fresh green or red chilli, deseeded and sliced

8–12 fresh basil leaves

salt

Pour a third of the coconut milk into a wok or heavy-based saucepan and stir in the curry paste. Simmer, stirring occasionally, for about 4 minutes, until oil is released and floats on the surface. Pour in remaining coconut milk and about ½ cup (125 ml/4 fl oz) water, then add sugar, fish sauce, mushrooms, zucchini, spring onions and chilli. Bring to the boil, reduce heat and simmer for about 5 minutes, until vegetables are tender. Stir in basil and check seasoning, adding salt if needed.

Green Curry of Tofu, Pea Eggplants & Straw Mushrooms

Serves 4–5

400 ml (13½ fl oz) coconut cream

1–1½ tablespoons green curry paste (page 235)

½ cup pea eggplants (or use ¾ cup green peas)

½ cup sliced bamboo shoots

12 canned straw mushrooms, cut in half

3 baby bok choy, slit in half

2 kaffir lime leaves (optional)

300 g (10½ oz) firm tofu, cut into 1.5-cm (½-in) cubes

3–4 teaspoons sugar

2 tablespoons (40 ml/1½ fl oz) fish sauce

salt

freshly squeezed lime juice (optional)

Heat half the coconut cream with the curry paste in a wok or saucepan and simmer, stirring, for 2–3 minutes. Add the remaining coconut cream and ¾ cup water and bring to the boil. Add the vegetables and lime leaves, and simmer gently for about 3 minutes. Add tofu and cook a further 2–3 minutes, then season to taste with sugar, fish sauce, salt, and lime juice (if using).

Seafood

Thailand borders the ocean and is criss-crossed with rivers and canals – so it's hardly surprising that seafood is important in Thai cuisine. As well as the catch from natural waterways, there's an enormous yield from the fish farms that dot the countryside. Fish and shellfish are very big business in this country, where prawns can be as fat as lobsters or as small as a baby's fingernail.

Whole fish is a popular item in restaurants, whether fried crisp and crunchy, or poached in fragrant broth. The tangy tastes of tamarind and lime juice, so popular in Thai cooking, are perfect complements to seafood, while pungent fish sauce reinforces the natural sea flavours.

< Steamed Ginger Squid (page 104)

Steamed Ginger Squid

Serves 4–6

12 small whole cleaned squid or 4 large squid tubes

1½ tablespoons very finely shredded fresh young ginger (or crushed ginger)

1 large fresh hot red chilli, deseeded and finely shredded

2 spring onions, cut into 2-cm (¾-in) pieces

2½ tablespoons (50 ml/ 1¾ fl oz) light soy sauce or fish sauce

Cut whole squid into rings (or leave whole if very small). If using large squid tubes, cut open and score the inside in a crosshatch pattern, then cut into 3-cm (1¼-in) squares.

Arrange squid in a shallow heatproof dish and scatter with the ginger, chilli and most of the spring onions (reserving some greens for garnish). Drizzle on the soy or fish sauce and set the dish in a steamer. Cook for about 7 minutes, until squid is tender.

Serve squid in the cooking dish, scattered with reserved spring onion.

Prawns with Black Pepper & Garlic

Serves 4

2 tablespoons (40 ml/1½ fl oz) oil

20 medium-sized raw (green) prawns, shelled and deveined but tails left on

3 spring onions, cut into 2-cm (¾-in) pieces

4 cloves garlic, chopped

2 teaspoons cracked black pepper

fish sauce or light soy sauce, to taste

pinch of sugar

⅓ cup fresh basil or coriander leaves

Heat oil in a wok and stir-fry prawns and spring onions for 1 minute. Add garlic and pepper, and cook for 30–40 seconds. Season to taste with fish sauce or soy sauce, and sugar, then add 2 tablespoons (40 ml/1½ fl oz) water. Stir-fry for another 20–30 seconds, then stir in basil or coriander leaves. Serve at once.

Grilled King Prawns with Tamarind Sauce

Serves 4

12 king prawns, shells left on

2 tablespoons (40 ml/1½ fl oz) oil, plus extra for brushing prawns

3 cloves garlic, chopped

1 medium-sized onion, finely diced

1–2 fresh hot red chillies, deseeded and diced

1 tablespoon tamarind paste

1½ tablespoons (30 ml/1 fl oz) fish sauce

2½ tablespoons (30 g/1 oz) palm sugar

With kitchen scissors, snip off the prawn legs, then cut deeply along the underside of the body and press open. Brush the cut sides with oil.

Heat a barbecue grill or non-stick pan to hot. Put prawns on, cut side down, and cook for 2 minutes, then turn and cook for another minute.

Meanwhile, heat oil in a wok over medium–high heat and stir-fry the garlic, onion and chillies for 1 minute. Add the tamarind paste, fish sauce, sugar and ½ cup (125 ml/4 fl oz) water and simmer, stirring, until it comes to the boil and the sugar dissolves. Taste for seasoning and adjust with a little more tamarind, fish sauce or sugar, or add a pinch of salt, as needed.

Transfer cooked prawns to a serving platter and spoon sauce over.

Stir-fried Prawns with Lemongrass & Kaffir Lime

Serves 4–6

3 large cloves garlic, peeled

5-cm (2-in) piece lemongrass, roughly chopped

2-cm (¾-in) slice fresh ginger

1 small fresh red chilli, deseeded

1 sprig fresh coriander, including root

2 spring onions (white parts only), roughly chopped

2 tablespoons (40 ml/1½ fl oz) oil

20–24 medium-sized raw (green) prawns, shelled and deveined

fish sauce, to taste

salt and freshly ground black pepper

2 kaffir lime leaves, very finely shredded

lime wedges, to serve

Place garlic, lemongrass, ginger, chilli, coriander and spring onions in a blender, spice grinder or food processor, and grind to a paste.

Heat oil in a wok and stir-fry the paste for about 1 minute. Add prawns and stir-fry over high heat until they turn pink. Season to taste with fish sauce, a pinch of salt and a generous grind of black pepper and continue to cook until prawns are cooked (1½–2 minutes). Fold in shredded lime leaves and serve at once, with lime wedges on the side.

Oyster-sauce Prawns

Serves 3–4

20 medium-sized raw (green) prawns, shelled and deveined but tails left on

1 spring onion, very thinly sliced

3 thin slices fresh ginger, finely shredded

2 tablespoons (40 ml/1½ fl oz) oyster sauce

1 teaspoon dark soy sauce

¾ teaspoon sugar

fresh coriander leaves, for garnish

Arrange prawns in a shallow heatproof dish and scatter the spring onion and ginger over. Mix 1 tablespoon oyster sauce with the soy sauce, sugar and 2 tablespoons (40 ml/1½ fl oz) water and pour evenly over the prawns. Set the dish in a steamer and cook for about 4–6 minutes, until prawns are just tender.

Serve prawns in the cooking dish, scattered with coriander and drizzled with remaining oyster sauce.

Whole Fried Fish in Ginger Sauce

Serves 3–4

900-g (2-lb) whole snapper

salt and freshly ground black pepper

about ½ cup (75 g/2½ oz) cornflour

oil for deep-frying

1 clove garlic, finely chopped

4 tablespoons fresh young ginger, very finely shredded

1 large fresh mild red chilli, deseeded and finely shredded

⅓ cup (80 ml/3 fl oz) rice vinegar

⅓ cup (75 g/2½ oz) sugar

1½ tablespoons fish sauce

1 spring onion (green part only), finely shredded

Heat oil to 180°C (360°F) in a wok or a large pan suitable for deep-frying.

With a sharp knife, make several deep slashes across each side of the fish. Season lightly with salt and pepper and coat with cornflour, pushing it into the cuts. Shake off excess.

Slide fish carefully into the oil and cook for about 6 minutes on each side, until golden-brown and crisp on the surface. Test for doneness by inserting a thin knife into the thickest part of the fish – it should easily penetrate to the bone and the flesh flake away. Carefully lift fish from the oil, hold over some paper towels for a moment to allow oil to drain off, then transfer to a serving plate. >

Pour oil from the wok, wipe surface and reheat. Add 2 tablespoons (40 ml/ 1½ fl oz) fresh oil and quickly sauté the garlic, ginger and chilli. Add vinegar, sugar and fish sauce, and bring to the boil. Mix 1 teaspoon cornflour with ½ cup (125 ml/4 fl oz) water and pour into the sauce, then add most of the spring onion greens and simmer for 1–2 minutes, stirring until sauce thickens and becomes translucent.

Spoon sauce over the fish and serve at once.

If young ginger cannot be obtained, use 1½ tablespoons crushed ginger instead.

Fish Cooked in Butter

Serves 4–5

400 g (14 oz) firm white fish, sliced

salt and freshly ground black pepper

½ cup (75 g/2½ oz) cornflour

120 g (4 oz) butter

4 thin slices fresh ginger, finely shredded

3 spring onions, cut into short lengths

1 clove garlic, sliced

1 fresh hot green chilli, deseeded and sliced

60 g (2 oz) sliced bamboo shoots

2 tomatoes, cut into wedges

1 tablespoon (20 ml/¾ fl oz) fish sauce

½ teaspoon sugar

Season fish with salt and pepper, then coat evenly with cornflour, shaking off the excess. Melt butter in a large pan over medium heat and cook the fish slices for about 40 seconds on each side, until golden-brown and almost cooked through. Carefully lift out of the pan onto a plate and set aside.

In the same pan, sauté the ginger, spring onions, garlic and chilli for about 1 minute, stirring. Add the bamboo shoots and tomatoes, and simmer for a few minutes, stirring.

Season with fish sauce and sugar, and add 3–4 tablespoons water to make a sauce. Simmer for 1–2 minutes, then return fish to the pan and heat gently in the sauce. Check seasonings and serve.

Fish in Banana-leaf Parcels

Serves 4–6

1 spring onion, finely chopped

1–1½ tablespoons red curry
paste (page 234)

2 teaspoons fish sauce

1 teaspoon sugar

3 tablespoons (60 ml/2 fl oz)
coconut cream

3 kaffir lime leaves, chopped

280 g (10 oz) soft-fleshed fish
(whiting, snapper, ling),
cubed

1–2 young fresh banana
leaves, cut into 15-cm ×
12-cm (6-in × 5-in) pieces

vegetable oil for brushing

Place spring onion, curry paste, fish sauce, sugar, coconut cream and lime leaves in a food processor and grind to a paste. Add the fish and process until fish is roughly chopped.

Soften the banana leaves by holding over a gas flame for a few seconds, then brush one side of each with oil. Preheat a barbecue grill or grill pan to hot.

Place a spoonful of fish mixture in the centre of each leaf, fold in the sides to cover the filling and secure the edges with toothpicks. Place parcels on the hot grill and cook for about 9 minutes, turning several times.

Banana leaves can be bought from Asian food stores. Alternatively, use cabbage leaves softened in boiling water and the centre rib trimmed away – wrap parcels in oiled aluminium foil before grilling.

Crisp-fried Fish with Chilli–lime Dressing

Serves 2–4

oil for deep-frying

1 × 900-g (2-lb) whole flat fish, such as John Dory or flounder

salt and ground white pepper

⅓ cup (50 g/1¾ oz) cornflour or arrowroot

crisp-fried basil leaves (page 245) (optional)

chilli–lime dressing (page 244)

Heat oil to 180°C (360°F) in a wok or a large pan suitable for deep-frying.

With a sharp knife, score both sides of the fish with a crosshatch. Season lightly with salt and white pepper and coat lightly with cornflour or arrowroot, pressing it into the cuts. Shake off excess flour.

Carefully slide fish into the oil and cook for about 5 minutes on each side, until golden-brown and cooked through. Test for doneness by inserting a thin knife into the thickest part of the fish – it should easily penetrate to the bone and the flesh flake away. Carefully lift fish from the oil and drain well.

Transfer fish to a platter and garnish with crisp-fried basil leaves if desired. Serve with the chilli–lime dressing on the side.

Steamed Whole Fish

1 × 900-g (2-lb) whole snapper or sea perch

6 small fresh bird's eye chillies (left whole) or 1 large fresh hot red chilli, deseeded and sliced

8 garlic chives, cut into 4-cm (1½-in) lengths

2 thin slices fresh ginger, finely shredded

juice of 1 lime and 3–4 strips of the zest

1 tablespoon (20 ml/¾ fl oz) fish sauce

1 kaffir lime leaf, shredded very finely (optional)

Make several diagonal slashes across both sides of the fish. Set fish on a heatproof plate and scatter with the chillies, garlic chives and ginger.

Place in a steamer or fish kettle and steam for 10 minutes. Add lime juice and zest, and fish sauce, then continue to steam until the fish is tender (2–3 more minutes). Test for doneness by inserting the point of a knife into the thickest part of the fish – the flesh should flake easily. Lift out of the steamer and scatter with the kaffir lime leaves. Serve at once.

Grilled Mackerel with Chilli & Tamarind Sauce

2 cloves garlic, peeled

1 sprig coriander, including root

1 thin slice fresh ginger

3 teaspoons fish sauce

1½ tablespoons (30 ml/1 fl oz) oil

4 mackerel steaks (or use swordfish)

TAMARIND SAUCE

1 small fresh hot red chilli, deseeded and finely chopped

1 tablespoon tamarind paste

2 tablespoons (30 g/1½ oz) palm sugar or soft brown sugar

1 tablespoon (20 ml/¾ fl oz) fish sauce

In a spice grinder or blender, grind the garlic, coriander, ginger and fish sauce to a paste. Add oil and blend again. Rub mixture over the fish and set aside to marinate for 20 minutes.

Heat a barbecue or hotplate to medium–high.

In a small saucepan, combine the tamarind sauce ingredients with ⅓ cup (80 ml/3 fl oz) water and simmer for 3–4 minutes. Taste and adjust with extra tamarind, sugar or fish sauce. Remove from heat and set aside.

Grill the fish for about 3 minutes on each side, or until cooked through, basting once with the tamarind sauce. Serve onto plates and spoon remaining sauce over.

Crab Cakes

Pu jaa

Serves 4

- **4 fresh sand crabs (about 375 g/13 oz each)**
- **1 large clove garlic, peeled**
- **1 sprig fresh coriander, including root**
- **1 slice fat bacon, finely chopped**
- **90 g (3 oz) pork mince**
- **1 large egg**
- **2 teaspoons fish sauce**
- **¼ cup fine dry breadcrumbs**
- **oil for deep-frying**
- **1 fresh red chilli, deseeded and finely shredded (optional)**
- **1 kaffir lime leaf, finely shredded (optional)**

Boil or steam the crabs for about 8 minutes, then set aside to drain and cool. When cool enough to handle, crack open, taking care not to break the body shells (these will be used for serving). Extract all of the meat and pick over to remove any fragments of shell.

Grind the garlic and coriander in a food processor or spice grinder. Add the bacon and chop briefly, then add the pork, egg, fish sauce, 1 tablespoon of the crumbs, and the crab meat. Process until reasonably smooth, then fill the mixture into the crab shells and cover with remaining breadcrumbs.

Heat oil to 170°C (340°F) in a wok or large saucepan suitable for deep-frying. Fry the crab cakes until golden-brown (about 3 minutes). Remove carefully and drain on paper towels.

Transfer crab cakes to plates, garnish with shredded red chilli and lime leaf (if using) and serve at once.

The crab cakes can also be made with shelled crab meat and cooked in small heatproof dishes. Omit the breadcrumb topping, brush tops with oil or butter, and steam or bake for 12–18 minutes.

Crab Stir-fried with Yellow Curry Paste

Serves 3–4

2–3 small sand crabs or blue swimmer crabs (about 900 g/2 lb in total)

2 tablespoons (40 ml/1½ fl oz) oil

3 spring onions, cut into 4-cm (1½-in) lengths

2–3 thin slices fresh ginger, finely shredded

1 tablespoon yellow curry paste

1 tablespoon (20 ml/¾ fl oz) fish sauce

salt and sugar, to taste

Crack open the crabs and remove the inedible parts. Rinse and drain.

With a cleaver or heavy knife chop each crab into four pieces, leaving legs attached. Cut large claws in half.

Heat oil in a wok and stir-fry the crab with the spring onion and ginger, until crab shells turn red. Add curry paste and fish sauce, and continue to stir-fry until the meat is cooked (about 2 minutes), adding a few tablespoons water to make a sauce if desired. Check for seasoning, adding salt and a large pinch of sugar, to taste.

Crayfish with Chilli & Lime Sauce

Gung phao

1 large or 2 small crayfish/ rock lobsters (about 1.5 kg/ 3 lb 5 oz in total)

4 lettuce leaves

CHILLI & LIME SAUCE

1 tablespoon (15 g/¾ oz) palm sugar or soft brown sugar

3 tablespoons (60 ml/2 fl oz) boiling water

3 teaspoons chopped garlic

2 teaspoons chopped fresh coriander leaves

2 teaspoons chopped fresh hot red chilli

juice of 1 large lime

Boil the crayfish in their shells for 12–20 minutes, depending on size, until the shell is red, tail is curled and flesh is firm. Plunge into iced water to prevent further cooking. Once cool, remove and drain well. Crack open the shell and extract the meat. Cut into medallions and arrange over the lettuce leaves.

To make the sauce, put sugar in a small bowl, add boiling water and stir to dissolve. Allow to cool, then add remaining ingredients, adjusting the quantities to suit your taste. Pour sauce into small dipping dishes and serve alongside the crayfish.

Steamed Mussels with Thai Herbs

Serves 4–6

1 kg (2 lb 3 oz) mussels in the shell

3 sprigs fresh coriander, including roots

1 stem lemongrass, thinly sliced

1-cm (⅜-in) piece galangal, sliced

1 fresh hot red chilli, deseeded and sliced

2 cloves garlic, sliced

2 spring onions, sliced

1 tablespoon (20 ml/¾ fl oz) fish sauce

Clean and debeard the mussels. Place in a saucepan with the remaining ingredients and 3 tablespoons (60 ml/2 fl oz) water. Cover tightly and bring to the boil. Reduce heat to low and steam for 2–4 minutes, until the shells open, shaking the pan frequently to help them along. Check after 4 minutes and transfer all the open mussels to a serving dish, then replace saucepan lid and cook the remainder for a minute or two longer. (If after 5 minutes of steaming some mussels remain unopened, it may be best to discard them.) Transfer the cooked mussels and the sauce to a large serving dish and serve at once.

Chicken, Duck & Quail

Chicken pairs perfectly with the sparkling spices, herbs and seasonings of Thai cuisine: the citrus sourness of kaffir lime, tamarind and lemongrass; the pungent scent of shrimp; the fiery flavour of chillies and pepper; the sweetness of palm sugar; and the salt tang of fish sauce. And some of the best chicken dishes are also the easiest to make – simply simmered with lemongrass or fried with garlic and pepper, oven-roasted with turmeric or stir-fried with ginger.

Duck and quail also cook beautifully the Thai way. Fresh quail and duck are readily available from poultry shops and Asian food stores, Chinese roast duck (perfect for dishes like the stir-fried duck with red curry paste) can be bought from Chinese take-away restaurants.

< Caramelised Chicken (page 128)

Caramelised Chicken

Serves 4

⅓ cup (75 g/2½ oz) white sugar

¼ cup (60 ml/2 fl oz) fish sauce

1 teaspoon freshly ground black pepper

1 large clove garlic, finely chopped

600 g (1 lb 5 oz) chicken thigh fillets (skin on), cut into 4-cm (1½-in) cubes

Pour sugar into a wok or saucepan and cook over medium heat, without stirring, until it melts and caramelises. Quickly remove from the heat before it burns and add the fish sauce, pepper and garlic (the sugar may harden into toffee). Add 2 tablespoons (40 ml/1½ fl oz) water and stir slowly until toffee melts.

Add chicken to the syrup and simmer over medium heat for about 3 minutes, stirring frequently. Cover and cook for a further 5 minutes, then remove lid and cook, stirring often, until the syrup forms a sticky glaze on the chicken.

Whole duck legs or cubed duck breast fillet can also be cooked this way, but will require a slightly longer final (covered) cooking time.

Fried Garlic & Pepper Chicken

Serves 4–6

1½ tablespoons cracked black pepper

1½ tablespoons crushed garlic

1½ teaspoons salt

1 tablespoon (20 ml/¾ fl oz) oil

1 kg (2 lb 3 oz) chicken pieces on the bone, skin on

oil for deep-frying

sweet chilli dipping sauce (page 243)

Make a paste with the first four ingredients. Add to a bowl with the chicken and rub the mixture all over the chicken pieces. Cover bowl with cling wrap and refrigerate for 1 hour.

Heat deep-frying oil to 180°C (360°F) in a wok or suitable deep pan. Pat chicken dry with paper towels and carefully place in the oil. Increase the heat slightly to keep the temperature steady and fry the chicken for 6–8 minutes, until golden-brown and cooked through. (For best results, do this in two or three batches.) Remove chicken with tongs and drain on paper towels.

Serve hot, with sweet chilli sauce for dipping.

ล Quail can be cooked this way: cut each in half before marinating.

Chicken with Lemongrass

Serves 3–4

450 g (1 lb) chicken thigh
fillets, each cut into three
pieces

8-cm (3-in) piece lemongrass,
finely sliced

3–8 fresh bird's eye chillies

2 tablespoons (40 ml/1½ fl oz)
fish sauce

2 teaspoons light soy sauce

1½ teaspoons sugar

2 tablespoons (40 ml/1½ fl oz)
oil

1 small cucumber, thinly
sliced

Place the chicken in a bowl with the lemongrass, chillies, sauces and sugar. Mix well. Cover and refrigerate for 2 hours, turning occasionally.

Heat oil in a non-stick frying pan. Tip the chicken and its marinade into the pan and sauté, turning often, until chicken is cooked through and golden-brown (about 7 minutes).

Serve chicken over sliced cucumber.

Bean Sprout & Shredded Chicken Stir-fry

Serves 4–6

2 tablespoons (40 ml/1½ fl oz) oil

150 g (5 oz) chicken breast fillet, shredded

1 spring onion or 8 garlic chives, cut into 2-cm (¾-in) pieces

1 large clove garlic, crushed

250 g (9 oz) fresh bean sprouts

1 tablespoon (20 ml/¾ fl oz) fish sauce

freshly ground black pepper

salt, to taste

2 tablespoons chopped fresh coriander

Heat oil in a wok over high heat and stir-fry chicken with spring onion (or chives) and garlic until chicken turns white (about 1 minute). Add bean sprouts and stir-fry for 1 minute or until tender. Season with fish sauce, pepper, and salt if needed, then stir in the coriander.

Oven-roasted Golden Chicken

4 large cloves garlic, peeled

1 teaspoon salt

1 teaspoon ground white pepper

½–1 teaspoon chilli paste

1⅓ teaspoons ground turmeric

2 × 900-g (2-lb) chickens, each cut in half along the backbone and flattened

CHILLI, GARLIC & VINEGAR DIPPING SAUCE

2 medium–hot red chillies, deseeded and finely chopped

4 cloves garlic, finely chopped

1 sprig fresh coriander, finely chopped

2 tablespoons (40 ml/1½ fl oz) vinegar

½ teaspoon salt

½ teaspoon sugar

Preheat the oven to 180°C (360°F). Set a roasting rack in an oven tray.

Make dipping sauce by combining all ingredients in a bowl.

Crush garlic in a mortar with the salt, pepper, chilli paste and turmeric. Rub mixture all over the chickens. Set chickens on the rack and roast for about 25 minutes, or until cooked through. (Check they are done by inserting a thin skewer into the thigh – the juices should run clear, not pink.)

Cut chickens into portions and serve with the dipping sauce.

The chicken could also be cooked on a barbecue over medium heat.

Spicy Braised Chicken Drumsticks

Serves 4–6

1 kg (2 lb 3 oz) chicken drumsticks

1 stem lemongrass, cut in half

2 thick slices galangal or ginger

3 kaffir lime leaves

1 medium-sized onion, quartered

4 cloves garlic, peeled

1–2 fresh hot red chillies, deseeded and cut in half

2 teaspoons shrimp paste

2 bunches coriander, including roots

2 tablespoons (40 ml/1½ fl oz) fish sauce

1 teaspoon sugar

salt

Place drumsticks in a saucepan with the lemongrass, galangal or ginger, and lime leaves. Add water to barely cover and simmer, uncovered, for 20 minutes.

Meanwhile, put onion, garlic, chilli, shrimp paste and coriander in a food processor, spice grinder or blender and grind to a paste. Stir in fish sauce and sugar.

Add spice mix to chicken and simmer over low heat until the drumsticks are very tender (about 25 minutes). Check seasoning, adding salt if needed, and serve.

Char-grilled Chicken

Kai yang

Serves 4

4 chicken marylands, skin on

1–2 teaspoons cracked black pepper

4 large cloves garlic, crushed

1–2 teaspoons chilli paste or crushed red chilli

2 tablespoons (40 ml/1½ fl oz) fish sauce

1 teaspoon sugar

1½ tablespoons (30 ml/1 fl oz) sesame oil

chilli, garlic and vinegar dipping sauce (page 133) or green papaya salad (page 67)

Prick chicken pieces all over with a sharp skewer. In a large bowl combine the pepper, garlic, chilli, fish sauce, sugar and sesame oil. Add chicken pieces to the bowl and rub the seasoning all over them. Cover the bowl with cling wrap and refrigerate for 3 hours, turning several times.

Heat a charcoal grill to medium–hot or an oven to 220°C (420°F).

Grill or bake the chicken, turning several times during cooking, until tender and succulent inside and well-crisped and browned on the outside (about 20 minutes).

Serve with the dipping sauce or salad.

Chicken & Water Chestnut Stir-fry

Serves 4–5

450 g (1 lb) chicken breast fillet, cut into 1-cm (⅜-in) cubes

2 tablespoons (40 ml/1½ fl oz) fish sauce

3 tablespoons (60 ml/2 fl oz) oil

4 garlic chives, cut into short lengths

3 thin slices fresh ginger, finely shredded

½ red capsicum, diced

½ small cucumber, diced (optional)

¾ teaspoon palm sugar

8 water chestnuts, sliced

salt and freshly ground black pepper

Marinate the chicken with half of the fish sauce and oil for 10 minutes.

Heat remaining oil in a wok and stir-fry the garlic chives, ginger and capsicum for 2 minutes. Add chicken and stir-fry until lightly browned. Add cucumber (if using), remaining fish sauce, sugar, water chestnuts and ½ cup (125 ml/4 fl oz) water. Simmer gently until chicken is tender (about 5 minutes). Check seasonings, adding salt and pepper to taste.

Stir-fried Chicken with Chillies & Green Capsicum

Serves 4–5

2 tablespoons (40 ml/1½ fl oz) oil

2–3 large cloves garlic, chopped

400 g (14 oz) chicken breast fillet, thinly sliced

2–4 large fresh mild red chillies, deseeded and sliced

1 green capsicum, cut into thin strips

1 small onion, cut into narrow wedges and layers separated

2 teaspoons light soy sauce or fish sauce

1½ tablespoons (30 ml/1 fl oz) oyster sauce

½ teaspoon palm sugar

12 fresh basil leaves (optional)

Heat oil in a wok and stir-fry the garlic and chicken until chicken is white. Remove to a plate. Reheat the wok, adding a little extra oil if needed, and stir-fry the chillies, capsicum and onion until softened (about 1½ minutes). Return the chicken to the pan and add the sauces, sugar and 2 tablespoons (40 ml/1½ fl oz) water to make a scant sauce. Stir until well mixed. Fold in the basil leaves (if using) and serve.

Chicken with Hot Chillies & Basil

Serves 4–6

3 cloves garlic, finely chopped

6 small fresh hot green chillies, chopped

2 spring onions, finely chopped

2 tablespoons (40 ml/1½ fl oz) oil

350 g (12 oz) coarsely minced chicken

2 large mild red chillies, deseeded and sliced

1 tablespoon (20 ml/¾ fl oz) oyster sauce

2–3 teaspoons fish sauce or light soy sauce

sugar, to taste

15 fresh basil leaves

Combine the garlic, green chillies and spring onions (reserving some of the greens for garnish) in a mortar or blender and grind to a coarse paste.

Heat oil in a wok over high heat and stir-fry the chilli paste for 1 minute. Add the minced chicken and the red chillies, and stir-fry until the chicken turns white. Season with the oyster sauce and fish or light soy sauce, and a large pinch of sugar. Add 2–3 tablespoons water and the basil leaves and mix well over high heat. Check seasoning, adjusting with extra sugar if needed.

Garnish with the reserved spring onion greens and serve.

Stir-fried Sesame Chicken

Serves 4

1½ tablespoons sesame seeds

2 tablespoons (40 ml/1½ fl oz) sesame oil

1 tablespoon (20 ml/¾ fl oz) vegetable oil

1 dried red chilli, deseeded and crumbled

3 cloves garlic, sliced

400 g (14 oz) chicken breast fillet, cut into 2-cm (¾-in) cubes

2 spring onions, cut into 2-cm (¾-in) pieces

1½ tablespoons (30 ml/1 fl oz) fish sauce

In a wok (without oil) toast the sesame seeds over medium heat until lightly golden-brown. Tip into a dish to cool.

Pour sesame oil and vegetable oil into the wok and heat until very hot. Fry chilli and garlic until lightly coloured. Add chicken and spring onions, and stir-fry for 2 minutes. Season with fish sauce and continue cooking over medium heat for about 1 minute more, until chicken is cooked. Stir in sesame seeds and serve.

ฮ์ You can use duck breast or lean pork instead of chicken.

Ginger Chicken

2 tablespoons (40 ml/1½ fl oz) oil

2–3 cloves garlic, chopped

400 g (14 oz) chicken breast fillet, cut into thin strips

3 spring onions, cut into 2-cm (¾-in) pieces

1 small onion, cut into narrow wedges and layers separated

2 tablespoons fresh young ginger, finely shredded

1 tablespoon (20 ml/¾ fl oz) light soy sauce or fish sauce

2 teaspoons rice wine or 1 cup diced pineapple

sugar, salt and ground white pepper, to taste

Heat oil in a wok and stir-fry garlic for 30 seconds. Add the chicken and stir-fry until it turns white. Add onions and ginger, and stir-fry for 2 minutes. Stir in soy or fish sauce, and rice wine or pineapple, add 1–2 pinches sugar, and salt and pepper to taste. Cook for a further minute, stirring, or until chicken is cooked.

If fresh young ginger is not available, use 3 teaspoons crushed ginger.

Chicken & Cashews

Serves 4

2 tablespoons (40 ml/1½ fl oz) oil

2 cloves garlic, chopped

400 g (14 oz) chicken breast fillet, cut into bite-size pieces

1 small onion, sliced

½–¾ cup roasted unsalted cashews

2 tablespoons (40 ml/1½ fl oz) fish sauce

1 teaspoon dark soy sauce (optional)

1 dried chilli, deseeded and very thinly sliced

fresh coriander or spring onion greens, for garnish

Heat oil in a wok and fry the garlic until lightly golden. Add chicken and onion and stir-fry until chicken is firm and white (about 2½ minutes). Stir in the cashews, season with fish sauce and soy sauce (if using) and add the chilli. Stir-fry for a further 1–2 minutes.

Pile onto a serving plate and garnish with coriander or spring onion greens.

Crisp-fried Quail with Pepper, Garlic & Soy

Serves 4–8

2 tablespoons (40 ml/1½ fl oz) dark soy sauce

2 tablespoons (40 ml/1½ fl oz) golden syrup (or use soft brown sugar)

6 cloves garlic, crushed

1½ teaspoons cracked white pepper

4 quail, each cut in half

oil for deep-frying

3 lettuce leaves, finely shredded

chilli, garlic and vinegar dipping sauce (page 133)

In a bowl, combine soy sauce, syrup or sugar, garlic and pepper, mixing well. Add the quail and turn several times to coat evenly. Leave to marinate for 20–40 minutes.

Heat oil to 180°C (360°F) in a wok or a saucepan suitable for deep-frying. Drain the quail and pat dry with paper towels, then deep-fry for 3–4 minutes, until golden-brown. Carefully lift out with tongs and drain well on paper towels.

Serve quail over shredded lettuce on a platter, with the dipping sauce on the side.

Crisp Roast Duck

1 × 1.8-kg (4-lb) duck

5-cm (2-in) piece fresh ginger

2 tablespoons (40 ml/1½ fl oz) dark soy sauce

1 tablespoon (20 ml/¾ fl oz) honey

1½ teaspoons Chinese five-spice powder

½ teaspoon ground white pepper

2 spring onions, chopped

sesame oil or vegetable oil, for brushing

Rinse the duck well, drain, then pour boiling water over the skin. Drain for 2 hours to allow the skin to dry. Preheat the oven to 160°C (320°F).

Grate half the ginger onto a piece of fine cloth and squeeze juice into a small bowl. Add soy sauce, honey, five-spice and pepper to the ginger juice and mix well. Paint this marinade liberally over the duck skin (reserve any leftover marinade). Place spring onions and remaining ginger in the cavity.

Brush a large piece of foil with oil, set the duck in the centre and wrap well. Place in an oven dish and bake for 2 hours. Remove foil and prick the skin to release fat. Brush with reserved marinade or dark soy, then with oil. Bake uncovered for 30 minutes, turning once, to crisp and colour the skin.

To serve, chop into bite-size pieces, cutting straight through the bones, or debone and tear meat into strips.

Duck Stir-fried with Red Curry Paste

Serves 3–4

½ Chinese roast duck

2 tablespoons (40 ml/1½ fl oz) oil

1 medium-sized onion, sliced

1 small zucchini, sliced

2–2½ teaspoons red curry paste (page 234)

1½ tablespoons (30 ml/1 fl oz) fish sauce

salt and sugar, to taste

fresh basil leaves, to serve

Debone the duck but do not remove the skin. Cut meat into bite-size pieces and, using a cleaver or heavy knife, chop the leg through the bone into three or four pieces.

Heat oil in a wok and stir-fry onion and zucchini until softened (about 2 minutes). Remove to a plate.

Reheat the wok and add the curry paste and a little more oil, if needed. Stir-fry the duck pieces very briefly (only 30–40 seconds) over very high heat, to warm the meat through. Return onion and zucchini to the wok and toss everything together over high heat. Add fish sauce and a pinch or two of salt and sugar to balance. Stir in basil leaves and serve.

Beef, Lamb & Pork

Full-flavoured braises like beef with star anise are just one of many alternatives to a Thai curry. Thai-style barbecued pork ribs, and sweet and sour pork, have a succulent stickiness. Some meat stir-fries are seasoned with soy sauce, bean paste and oyster sauce in the Chinese way, while others pack a flavour punch with curry pastes, black pepper, fish sauce and garlic as the prime seasonings. Beef, pork and lamb are interchangeable in most Thai stir-fries, so feel free to swap the meat used in any of these recipes. You can also substitute fish sauce for soy sauce, and vice versa.

Serve stir-fries and braised meat dishes with steamed white rice, or try sticky rice (page 11) for something different. Offer authentic side dishes such as hot chilli sauces, wedges of hard-boiled egg, and slices of cucumber or pineapple, and use generous quantities of fresh herbs, shredded chilli or roasted peanuts for garnish.

< Stir-fried Beef in Oyster Sauce with Mushrooms (page 154)

Stir-fried Beef in Oyster Sauce with Mushrooms

Serves 4

400 g (14 oz) beef rump or sirloin, very thinly sliced

2 teaspoons cornflour

2 teaspoons fish sauce

2 teaspoons dark soy sauce

2½ tablespoons (50 ml/ 1¾ fl oz) oil

1 large clove garlic, chopped

2 tablespoons (40 ml/1½ fl oz) oyster sauce

1 teaspoon palm sugar

1½ cups sliced fresh mushrooms (oyster, straw, enoki, Swiss brown)

1 large fresh red chilli, deseeded and sliced

1 spring onion, sliced

Mix beef with the cornflour and fish and soy sauces. Leave for 10 minutes to marinate.

Heat oil in a wok over very high heat and stir-fry the beef and garlic for about 1½ minutes. Add half the oyster sauce and a few tablespoons water, along with the sugar, mushrooms, chilli and spring onion (reserving some of the greens). Stir-fry until mushrooms are tender and meat cooked (about 1½ minutes). Pour in remaining oyster sauce, then check seasoning, adjusting with extra sugar if needed.

Garnish with reserved spring onion greens to serve.

Beef with Chilli
& Kaffir Lime Leaves

Serves 4–5

2½ tablespoons (50 ml/
   1¾ fl oz) oil

2 cloves garlic, chopped

2–5 bird's eye chillies (to taste)

1 medium-sized red onion,
   sliced

400 g (14 oz) beef fillet, very
   thinly sliced

1½ tablespoons (30 ml/1 fl oz)
   fish sauce

1 tablespoon (20 ml/¾ fl oz)
   oyster sauce

½–1 teaspoon sugar

4–5 kaffir lime leaves, very
   finely shredded

Heat oil in a wok over high heat and stir-fry the garlic, chillies and onion for about 1½ minutes. Add the beef and stir-fry over very high heat for about 1½ minutes, until meat changes colour. Season with fish and oyster sauces, and sugar, and stir in the shredded lime leaves. Serve immediately.

Chilli Beef & Basil

Serves 4–5

400 g (14 oz) beef rump or sirloin (or use lean lamb)

2½ tablespoons (50 ml/ 1¾ fl oz) oil

1 large onion, thinly sliced

3–4 cloves garlic, chopped

2 large fresh hot green chillies, deseeded and sliced

1 large fresh hot red chilli, deseeded and sliced

1½ tablespoons (30 ml/1 fl oz) fish sauce

½–1 teaspoon sugar

10–15 fresh basil leaves

Cut the meat into paper-thin slices, then stack these together and cut into narrow strips.

Heat oil in a wok over high heat and stir-fry onion, garlic and chillies for about 1½ minutes, until softened. Add beef and stir-fry over very high heat for about 1½ minutes. Season with fish sauce and sugar, add about 2 tablespoons (40 ml/1½ fl oz) water, then sauté briefly. Stir in the basil leaves and serve.

Beef Braised with Star Anise

Serves 4–6

1 kg (2 lb 3 oz) braising beef, cut into 2-cm (¾-in) cubes

4 star anise

1 cinnamon stick

¼ cup (60 ml/2 fl oz) light soy sauce or fish sauce

1 tablespoon (15 g/½ oz) palm sugar or soft brown sugar

2.5-cm (1-in) piece galangal (optional)

2 spring onions, chopped (whites and greens kept separate)

2 tablespoons (30 g/1 oz) cornflour (optional)

150 g (5 oz) fresh bean sprouts

5 lettuce leaves, chopped

In a heavy-based saucepan combine the beef, spices, soy or fish sauce, sugar, galangal (if using) and spring onion whites. Add water to barely cover the meat and bring to the boil. Skim off any impurities that rise to the surface. Reduce heat and simmer gently, uncovered, for about 1 hour, turning the meat and skimming the surface from time to time. If desired, thicken sauce by adding cornflour mixed with ⅓ cup (80 ml/3 fl oz) cold water, then simmering for 4–5 minutes, stirring.

Blanch the bean sprouts and lettuce in boiling water, drain and divide between 4–6 deep bowls. Ladle on the beef and sauce, and garnish with the spring onion greens.

Minced Beef & Bamboo Shoot Stir-fry

2½ tablespoons (50 ml/1¾ fl oz) vegetable or sesame oil

2–3 cloves garlic, chopped

350 g (12 oz) beef mince (or use lamb)

90 g (3 oz) bamboo shoots, finely diced

½ red capsicum, finely diced

1 small onion, finely diced

1 fresh hot red chilli, deseeded and chopped

2 tablespoons (40 ml/1½ fl oz) fish sauce

1 teaspoon sugar

salt and freshly ground black pepper

1 small iceberg or soft-leaf lettuce (optional)

Heat oil in a wok and stir-fry the garlic for 20 seconds. Add beef and stir-fry until lightly browned, then add the diced vegetables and the chilli, and stir-fry for about 2 minutes, until well cooked. Add the fish sauce and sugar, seasoning with salt and pepper if needed.

Serve the stir-fry with rice, or as portions wrapped in lettuce leaves.

Stir-fried Lamb with Pepper & Garlic

Serves 4–6

3 tablespoons (60 ml/2 fl oz) oil

450 g (1 lb) lean lamb (or use lean pork), cut into thin strips

4 large cloves garlic, chopped

1–2 large fresh hot red chillies, deseeded and sliced

2–2½ teaspoons cracked black pepper

3 teaspoons light soy sauce or fish sauce

salt

2–3 tablespoons chopped fresh coriander leaves

Heat oil in a wok over medium heat and stir-fry the meat until almost cooked (about 4 minutes). Remove to a plate.

Pour half the oil from the wok, reheat, then stir-fry the garlic and chilli until garlic is lightly golden. Return meat to the wok, add pepper, soy or fish sauce, 2–3 tablespoons water, and a pinch of salt. Stir-fry until well mixed, stir in coriander leaves, and serve.

Stir-fry of Lamb with Garlic Shoots & Chilli

Serves 3–4

3 tablespoons (60 ml/2 fl oz) oil

300 g (10½ oz) lamb back strap or leg steaks, cut into thin slices

1 large fresh hot red chilli, deseeded and sliced

100 g (3½ oz) garlic shoots (or garlic chives), cut into 2-cm (¾-in) lengths

½ red capsicum, sliced

3 tablespoons (60 ml/2 fl oz) oyster sauce

½ teaspoon sugar

Heat a wok with half the oil over high heat and stir-fry the lamb and chilli until meat is browned (about 1½ minutes). Remove to a plate.

Reheat the wok with remaining oil and stir-fry the garlic shoots (or chives) and capsicum for about 1½ minutes. Add the oyster sauce and sugar, return meat to the pan and mix well. Stir in 3 tablespoons water and stir-fry for about 40 seconds.

Sweet & Sour Pork

Serves 4–6

650 g (1 lb 7 oz) pork belly, cut into thin strips

2 teaspoons grated fresh ginger

1½ tablespoons (30 ml/1 fl oz) fish sauce

1 cup (150 g/5 oz) cornflour

3 tablespoons (60 ml/2 fl oz) vinegar

3 tablespoons (45 g/2¼ oz) palm sugar or soft brown sugar

¾ cup diced canned pineapple (juice from the can reserved)

1½ teaspoons chopped garlic

¾ teaspoon cracked black pepper (optional)

3 tablespoons (60 ml/2 fl oz) tomato sauce

½ cup (125 ml/4 fl oz) chicken stock or water

2 teaspoons cornflour

oil for deep-frying

1 green capsicum, diced

1 large fresh red chilli, deseeded and sliced

1 small onion, diced

Place pork in a bowl and add the ginger and half the fish sauce. Mix well and leave to marinate for 1 hour. Remove pork from marinade and coat each piece with cornflour.

In a bowl mix the vinegar, sugar, pineapple juice, garlic, pepper and tomato sauce. Stir in chicken stock or water, and cornflour, and set aside. >

Heat oil to 180°C (360°F) in a wok or a large saucepan suitable for deep-frying. Fry the pork for about 8 minutes, turning frequently, until golden. Remove pork and drain on paper towels.

Pour all but a few teaspoons oil from the wok, then reheat. Stir-fry the capsicum, chilli and onion until softened (about 2½ minutes). Pour in the prepared sauce, add pineapple pieces and simmer, stirring frequently, for about 5 minutes. Return pork to wok and simmer gently for 2–3 minutes, then serve.

Sliced Pork Stir-fried with Red Curry Paste

Serves 4–5

400 g (14 oz) lean pork, very thinly sliced

1–2 tablespoons red curry paste (page 234)

3 tablespoons (60 ml/2 fl oz) oil

3 tablespoons (60 ml/2 fl oz) coconut cream

1 large fresh red chilli, deseeded and sliced

2 kaffir lime leaves, torn in half

1½ tablespoons (30 ml/1 fl oz) fish sauce

2–3 teaspoons sugar

fresh basil or coriander leaves, to serve

Place pork in a bowl with the curry paste and stir to coat. Heat oil in a wok and stir-fry the pork for about 2 minutes over high heat, until lightly browned. Add the coconut cream, chilli and lime leaves, and stir-fry until the liquid has almost all evaporated (about 2 minutes). Stir in ⅓ cup (80 ml/ 3 fl oz) water, add the fish sauce and sugar, and simmer briefly. Check seasonings and add more fish sauce or sugar if needed.

Stir in basil or coriander leaves just before serving.

If desired, add cooked green beans or baby corn in the last 2 minutes of cooking.

Barbecued Pork Ribs

Serves 6

850 g (1 lb 14 oz) meaty pork spare ribs

1 bunch coriander, including roots, finely chopped

3–4 cloves garlic, chopped

2 tablespoons (40 ml/1½ fl oz) oyster sauce

1½ tablespoons (30 ml/1 fl oz) fish sauce

1 teaspoon sugar

1½ teaspoons cracked black pepper

Cut each pork rib in half and place in a bowl. Add coriander, garlic, oyster and fish sauces, sugar and pepper. Mix well, cover and refrigerate for 3–4 hours, turning occasionally.

Heat a barbecue or grill to medium–hot. Cook the pork ribs for about 15 minutes, turning often, until well browned on the surface and meat is tender.

Alternatively, you can cook the ribs in a 180°C (360°F) oven for about 45 minutes.

Spicy Minced Pork

Serves 4–5

4 cloves garlic, peeled

3 coriander roots, chopped

1 large fresh hot red chilli, deseeded and sliced

2 tablespoons (40 ml/1½ fl oz) oil

400 g (14 oz) pork mince

5–6 fresh bird's eye chillies

2 tablespoons (40 ml/1½ fl oz) fish sauce

1 tablespoon (20 ml/¾ fl oz) oyster sauce

1 teaspoon sugar

12 fresh basil leaves

In a mortar or spice grinder, grind the garlic, coriander roots and sliced chilli to a paste.

Heat the oil in a wok over high heat and fry the paste for 1 minute. Add pork and bird's eye chillies, and stir-fry for about 5 minutes, until the pork is well browned. Add the fish and oyster sauces, sugar and about ¾ cup (180 ml/6 fl oz) water and simmer, stirring occasionally, until pork is tender and liquid has evaporated (about 8 minutes).

Check seasonings, adding more fish sauce or sugar if needed, then stir in basil leaves and serve.

Crisp Pork with Bean Sprouts

Serves 5–6

600 g (1 lb 5 oz) pork belly in one piece, with skin on

oil for deep-frying

1 tablespoon (20 ml/¾ fl oz) sesame oil (optional)

180 g (6½ oz) fresh bean sprouts

2 cloves garlic, finely chopped

1½ tablespoons (30 ml/1 fl oz) fish sauce or oyster sauce

fresh coriander sprigs, for garnish

Place pork in a saucepan with enough lightly salted water to cover. Bring to the boil, then reduce heat and simmer for about 1 hour, until the meat is very tender.

Leave pork in the cooking liquid until cool enough to handle, then transfer to a colander to drain. Cut meat into slices 1 cm (⅜ in) thick and leave on paper towels to dry.

Heat deep-frying oil to 180°C (360°F) in a wok and add the sesame oil (if using). Fry the sliced pork for about 7 minutes, until skin is golden-brown. Remove from the oil with tongs or a slotted spoon and drain well on paper towels. Cut pork into bite-size chunks.

Pour all but a few teaspoons of oil from the wok and reheat. Stir-fry the bean sprouts and garlic for about 1½ minutes, then remove to a plate. Reheat the wok with a little extra oil and stir-fry the chunks of pork for about 1 minute, until crisp. Return the bean sprouts and garlic to the wok, season with fish or oyster sauce, and toss to combine.

Serve garnished with coriander sprigs.

Pork Stir-fry with Crisp Young Ginger

Serves 4–5

- 3 teaspoons sesame oil
- 1 teaspoon cornflour
- 350 g (12 oz) lean pork, cut into very thin strips
- 2½ tablespoons (50 ml/ 1¾ fl oz) vegetable oil
- 2 tablespoons fresh young ginger, finely shredded
- 1½ tablespoons (30 ml/1 fl oz) fish sauce
- 2 teaspoons light soy sauce
- sugar, to taste

Combine sesame oil and cornflour in a bowl. Add pork and stir to coat. Set aside for 20 minutes, stirring several times.

Heat oil in a wok and stir-fry the ginger until quite crisp. Add the pork strips and stir-fry until white and firm. Season with fish and soy sauces, and add a little sugar, to taste.

Braised Five-spice Pork

Serves 6

1½ tablespoons Chinese five-spice powder

4 cloves garlic, finely chopped

4 tablespoons oil

1 kg (2 lb 3 oz) pork belly or bacon, cut into 4-cm (1½-in) cubes

½ cup (125 ml/4 fl oz) light soy sauce

2 tablespoons (40 ml/1½ fl oz) oyster sauce

2 tablespoons (30 g/1½ oz) palm sugar or soft brown sugar

2 tablespoons (30 g/1 oz) cornflour (optional)

salt

Combine the five-spice and garlic with half the oil. Rub into the pork (or bacon) and set aside for 1 hour to marinate.

Heat remaining oil in a wok or heavy-based saucepan over high heat and brown the meat, stirring constantly. Add the soy and oyster sauces, sugar, and enough water to cover. Bring to the boil, reduce heat and simmer gently for 45–60 minutes, until pork is very tender. (Thicken the sauce, if desired, by adding cornflour mixed with enough cold water to make a smooth paste.)

Check seasonings, adjusting with salt and sugar to taste. Serve.

Vegetables & Tofu

Common vegetables grown in Thailand include snake beans, asparagus, asparagus beans, Chinese celery, and a spinach-like leaf called *bai dtamleung* – not to mention various cabbages and other Asian greens. And there's all manner of edible fungi – from crinkly black cloud ears to straw mushrooms. Then there are crunchy bean sprouts, bamboo shoots, white and yellow sweet potatoes, and eggplants of many shapes, colours and sizes.

Vegetables may be curried, stir-fried, grilled, steamed, or simmered in coconut milk. A platter of decoratively carved vegetables (page 20) is the traditional partner to the many pungent or spicy dips served as snacks.

Vegetarians can replace fish sauce with soy sauce, and omit shrimp paste and other seafood ingredients from curry pastes. Tofu adds texture and protein to vegetable stir-fries and curries.

< Stir-fry of Vegetables & Cashews (page 176)

Stir-fry of Vegetables & Cashews

Serves 4–6

⅓ cup (80 ml/3 fl oz) oil

⅓ cup raw cashew nuts

1 small onion, diced

½ red capsicum, diced

450 g (1 lb) vegetables (sliced beans, carrot, baby corn, bamboo shoots, mushrooms, cauliflower and broccoli florets)

3 thin slices fresh ginger, finely shredded

1 fresh hot red chilli, deseeded and finely shredded

1½ tablespoons (30 ml/1 fl oz) fish sauce or light soy sauce

1½ teaspoons cornflour

salt and freshly ground black pepper

sugar, to taste

Heat the oil in a wok and fry the cashews until golden-brown. Remove with a slotted spoon and set aside. Pour all but a few teaspoons oil from the wok. Reheat the wok and stir-fry the onion for 1 minute. Add prepared vegetables (except baby corn, bamboo shoots, mushrooms and bean sprouts) and stir-fry for 1½ minutes. Add remaining vegetables, ginger, chilli and fish or soy sauce and stir-fry for 1–2 minutes.

Mix the cornflour with enough cold water to make a smooth paste and pour into the wok. Cook, stirring, until sauce thickens and becomes translucent. Check seasonings, adding salt, pepper and a pinch of sugar. Stir in cashews and serve.

Stir-fried Beans & Corn with Chilli & Basil

Serves 4

18 green beans or 4 snake beans, cut into 5-cm (2-in) pieces

1 cup corn kernels or sliced baby corn

2 tablespoons (40 ml/1½ fl oz) oil

1–2 fresh hot red chillies, deseeded and roughly chopped

2–3 cloves garlic, peeled

1 small bunch holy or sweet basil, leaves torn

3–4 teaspoons fish sauce

about 1 teaspoon caster sugar

Bring 1 cup (250 ml/8½ fl oz) water to the boil in a wok or saucepan and cook beans and corn for 3 minutes. Tip into a colander to drain.

Reheat wok with oil and fry the chillies and garlic for about 40 seconds, until fragrant. Add vegetables and stir-fry for about 1 minute, until coated with the garlic and chilli. Stir in basil leaves, fish sauce and sugar to taste. Stir-fry briefly to combine, then serve.

Water Spinach Stir-fried with Garlic & Shrimp Paste

Serves 4–6

1 bunch water spinach or English spinach (or ½ bunch silverbeet)

2 tablespoons (40 ml/1½ fl oz) oil

3–4 cloves garlic, chopped

¾ teaspoon shrimp paste, crumbled

100 ml (3½ fl oz) chicken stock or water

1½ tablespoons (30 ml/1 fl oz) fish sauce or light soy sauce

Cut water spinach into 10-cm (4-in) lengths. (For English spinach, trim off and discard the stems. For silverbeet, shred leaves and slice stems on the diagonal.)

Heat oil in a wok and stir-fry the garlic and shrimp paste for 20 seconds. Add spinach and stir-fry until coated with oil. (If using silverbeet, cook stems for 1 minute before adding leaves.) Pour in stock or water and add soy or fish sauce. Cook over high heat, stirring and turning continually, until tender (1½–2 minutes).

Sweet & Tangy Vegetables

2 tablespoons (40 ml/1½ fl oz) oil

2 cloves garlic, crushed

1 small carrot, sliced

½ red capsicum, diced

1 medium-sized salad onion or red onion, sliced

1 small cucumber, deseeded and sliced

2 barely ripe tomatoes, cut into thin wedges

2 thick slices fresh pineapple, cubed

2 tablespoons (40 ml/1½ fl oz) fish sauce

1 tablespoon (15 g/¾ oz) palm sugar or soft brown sugar

salt

freshly squeezed lime or lemon juice

Heat oil in a wok and stir-fry the garlic, carrot, capsicum and onion until softened (about 2 minutes). Add cucumber, tomatoes and pineapple, and stir-fry until softened (about 1½ minutes). Season with fish sauce and sugar, stirring well. Taste, add salt if needed and squeeze in some lime or lemon juice.

Mushrooms & Chinese Cabbage in Oyster Sauce

Serves 4–6

2 tablespoons (40 ml/1½ fl oz) oil

1½ cups sliced fresh mushrooms (straw, button, oyster, shiitake)

2 large cloves garlic, chopped

1 spring onion, sliced

400 g (14 oz) Chinese cabbage, chopped

3½ tablespoons (70 ml/ 2½ fl oz) oyster sauce

½ teaspoon sugar

Heat the oil in a wok over very high heat and stir-fry mushrooms, garlic and spring onion for about 40 seconds. Add the cabbage and stir-fry for 1 minute, then cover and steam for about 2 minutes, until tender. Remove lid and stir in about half the oyster sauce, plus the sugar. Cook, stirring often, for another minute.

Transfer to a serving plate and drizzle with remaining oyster sauce.

Vegetables Fried in Coconut Batter

Serves 6

½ cup (75 g/2½ oz) self-raising flour

½ cup (75 g/2½ oz) rice flour

¾ cup coconut cream

1½ teaspoons salt

1 teaspoon crushed chilli or chilli powder

1 teaspoon crushed garlic

oil for deep-frying

180 g (6½ oz) pumpkin, cut into 2.5-cm (1-in) chunks

180 g (6½ oz) sweet potato, cut into 2.5-cm (1-in) chunks

12 green beans, cut in half

6 button mushrooms, cut in half

chilli, garlic and vinegar dipping sauce (page 133), to serve (optional)

crisp-fried basil leaves (page 245), for garnish (optional)

Make a batter by mixing the sifted flours with the coconut cream, salt and chilli, and adding enough cold water to achieve a creamy consistency.

Heat oil to 170°C (340°F) in a wok or a large pan suitable for deep-frying. Place sheets of paper towel on a wire rack.

Drag vegetables one by one through the batter to coat lightly, then carefully slide into the oil. Fry until golden-brown and cooked through (about 3 minutes for pumpkin and sweet potato, 2 minutes for beans and mushrooms). Remove with a slotted spoon and drain on the paper towels. Serve hot, with dipping sauce on the side and/or garnished with crisp-fried basil leaves.

Mushroom Stir-fry with Eggs

Serves 4–6

8 dried or fresh shiitake
mushrooms

2 pieces dried black cloud ear
(wood ear) fungus

2 tablespoons (40 ml/1½ fl oz)
oil

1–2 fresh hot red chillies,
deseeded and chopped

1–2 cloves garlic, chopped

2 spring onions, cut into 2-cm
(¾-in) lengths

2 eggs

1 tablespoon (20 ml/¾ fl oz)
fish sauce

salt and freshly ground black
pepper

2 tablespoons chopped fresh
coriander

Pour boiling water over dried shiitakes and fungus and leave to soak for about 25 minutes, to soften. Drain well, trim away any woody parts and chop finely. (Chop fresh shiitakes, if using.)

Heat oil in a wok over high heat and stir-fry the chillies and garlic for 20 seconds. Add spring onions, shiitakes and fungus, and stir-fry for about 40 seconds. Beat eggs with fish sauce and pour into the wok. Reduce heat to low–medium and stir gently until eggs are barely set. Check seasoning, adding salt and pepper to taste. Stir in coriander and serve.

Tofu & Vegetables in Soy Sauce

Serves 4–6

250 g (9 oz) soft tofu, cut into 2.5-cm (1-in) cubes

¾ cup (110 g/4 oz) cornflour

oil for deep-frying

2–3 cloves garlic, chopped

3 cups mixed vegetables (sliced carrot, green beans, baby corn, mushrooms, cauliflower florets)

2 spring onions, cut into 2-cm (¾-in) pieces

2 tablespoons (40 ml/1½ fl oz) light soy sauce

sugar, to taste

salt and freshly ground black pepper

Carefully coat the tofu with cornflour.

Heat oil to 180°C (360°F) in a wok or a large pan suitable for deep-frying. Fry the tofu until golden (about 1½ minutes). Lift out and drain well on paper towels.

Pour all but a few teaspoons of oil from the wok. Reheat wok and fry garlic briefly. Add vegetables and spring onions and stir-fry for 2–3 minutes, until almost cooked. Season with soy sauce and a pinch of sugar. Mix 3 teaspoons cornflour with ¾ cup (180 ml/6 fl oz) cold water and pour into the pan. Bring to the boil and stir until sauce thickens. Check seasoning, adding salt and pepper to taste. Return tofu to the pan and warm gently in the sauce.

Vegetable Omelette Parcels

1½ tablespoons (30 ml/1 fl oz) oil

1 small onion, diced

½ green capsicum, diced

1 tomato, deseeded and diced

150 g (5 oz) fresh bean sprouts

fish sauce or light soy sauce

salt and freshly ground pepper

4 large eggs

fresh coriander leaves, to serve

fresh hot red chilli, deseeded and finely shredded

Heat oil in a wok and sauté the onion and capsicum until softened (about 1½ minutes). Add tomato and bean sprouts, and stir-fry until tomato is pulpy. Season to taste with fish sauce or soy sauce, salt and pepper. Set aside.

Beat eggs with 2 tablespoons (40 ml/1½ fl oz) water and a pinch of salt. Heat a non-stick frying pan or omelette pan over medium heat. Pour in a quarter of the egg mixture, tilting the pan so eggs form a large, thin omelette. Cook until lightly browned underneath, then flip to cook the other side. Place a quarter of the vegetables in the centre and fold in the sides to make a neat parcel. Turn to brown the underside, then slide onto a plate. Cover loosely with foil while you cook another three omelettes. Garnish with coriander and chilli to serve.

Chicken, pork or prawn mince can be added to the filling – add to the wok before you add the tomato and bean sprouts.

Tofu in Tamarind Sauce

Serves 4

about 100 ml (3½ fl oz) oil

3 cloves garlic, sliced

1–2 fresh hot red chillies, deseeded and sliced

350 g (12 oz) firm tofu, cut into cubes

4 tablespoons (60 g/3 oz) palm sugar or soft brown sugar

1½ tablespoons tamarind paste

⅓ cup (80 ml/3 fl oz) fish sauce

2–3 tablespoons sliced spring onion greens

Heat oil in a wok and fry the garlic and chillies until lightly browned. Remove with a mesh strainer and set aside. In the same oil, fry the tofu over medium heat until lightly browned (about 1½ minutes), then lift out and drain on paper towels.

Pour off all but a few teaspoons of the oil, then reheat wok and stir in the sugar, tamarind, fish sauce and 3–4 tablespoons water. Simmer, stirring often, until sugar dissolves and liquid becomes slightly syrupy (about 2 minutes). Return tofu to the wok and simmer in the sauce for 2–3 minutes, until glazed. Add the fried chilli and garlic and spring onion greens, toss lightly and serve.

Rice & Noodles

Rice is an essential part of every Thai meal. Jasmine rice, a delicately fragrant long-grain white rice, is the preferred rice to eat plain; it is steamed and served alongside curries or stir-fries. Both jasmine and glutinous rice may be stir-fried or simmered with other ingredients, to make tasty small meals, snacks or side dishes.

Noodles are thought to have been introduced to Thailand by immigrants from southern China, and today they form a large part of the Thai diet. Noodles are usually eaten as a snack between meals, or as a breakfast dish. Rice noodles, bean-threads and egg noodles are all used, and most are available fresh or dried. Rice-noodle sheets may be used as wrappers or cut into wide, ribbon-like noodles. The noodle dishes here can be eaten on their own as a light meal, or served alongside curries or other dishes as part of a dinner menu.

< Pork & Sausage Rice Pot (page 194)

Pork & Sausage Rice Pot

3 dried shiitake mushrooms

1½ tablespoons (30 ml/1 fl oz) oil

2–3 cloves garlic, chopped

1 teaspoon finely chopped fresh ginger

2 Chinese sausages (Thai *kun chiang*), sliced

250 g (9 oz) lean pork, cut into small cubes

2 cups jasmine rice

2 tablespoons (40 ml/1½ fl oz) oyster sauce

2 tablespoons (40 ml/1½ fl oz) light soy sauce or fish sauce

Soak the dried mushrooms in hot water for about 25 minutes, then strain through a fine sieve, reserving the liquid. Pick out the stems and slice caps thinly.

Preheat the oven to 180°C (360°F).

Heat oil in a wok and sauté the garlic and ginger until lightly golden. Add sausages and pork, and stir-fry until lightly browned. Add sliced mushrooms and the rice, and stir until rice is coated with oil. Stir in the sauces, then transfer to a clay pot or casserole dish. Make reserved mushroom stock up to 3 cups (750 ml/25 fl oz) with lukewarm water or chicken stock. Pour stock over the rice, stir, cover tightly and cook in the oven until rice has absorbed all of the liquid and is plump and tender (about 20 minutes).

Poached Chicken & Rice

Serves 4

450 g (1 lb) chicken thigh
   fillets

4–5 thin slices fresh ginger

1 teaspoon salt

2 tablespoons (40 ml/1½ fl oz)
   oil

2–3 cloves garlic, crushed

2 cups jasmine rice

1 small cucumber, sliced

SOY & GINGER SAUCE

2 teaspoons chilli bean paste,
   crushed

2 tablespoons (40 ml/1½ fl oz)
   light soy sauce

1 tablespoon (20 ml/¾ fl oz)
   vinegar

2 teaspoons crushed ginger

sugar, to taste

To make the sauce, simply mix all ingredients together.

Place chicken in a saucepan with water to cover, ginger and salt. Bring to the boil, then simmer gently for about 25 minutes, until tender. Remove and set aside to cool, reserving the stock.

Heat oil in a heavy-based saucepan and fry garlic briefly. Pour in the rice and stir to coat, then strain in 3 cups (750 ml/25 fl oz) of the reserved stock. Cover, bring to the boil, then reduce heat and steam the rice until tender (about 15 minutes). Meanwhile, cut chicken into bite-size pieces.

Pile rice onto a serving platter, with the chicken and cucumber alongside. Serve with the sauce on the side for dipping.

Golden Chicken Rice

Serves 4–6

1 kg (2 lb 3 oz) chicken pieces on the bone (e.g. thighs, legs and wings)

2 tablespoons (40 ml/1½ fl oz) oil

4 cloves garlic, chopped

2½ cups jasmine rice

1 stem lemongrass, cut into 4–5 pieces

1¼ teaspoons ground turmeric

2 teaspoons chicken stock powder

With a cleaver or heavy knife, chop each chicken piece into three, cutting through the bone.

Heat oil in a heavy saucepan with a lid and gently brown the garlic. Add rice, lemongrass, turmeric and stock powder, and mix well. Add the chicken pieces and 3 cups (750 ml/25 fl oz) water, cover tightly and bring to the boil. Reduce heat to very low and steam gently for about 25 minutes, without stirring.

Remove the lid and give the rice a stir – it should be plump and tender and the liquid completely absorbed. Serve in deep bowls.

Thai Fried Rice with Pineapple

Serves 6

2 cups jasmine rice

4 tablespoons (80 ml/3 fl oz) oil

2 eggs, beaten

1 large clove garlic, chopped

2 spring onions, chopped

¼ red capsicum, chopped

1 tablespoon dried shrimp

120 g (4 oz) small raw (green) shelled prawns (or use diced chicken or tofu)

2–3 slices canned or fresh pineapple, diced

2 tablespoons (40 ml/1½ fl oz) fish sauce

1 tablespoon (20 ml/¾ fl oz) sweet chilli sauce

salt and freshly ground black pepper

1 fresh hot red chilli, deseeded and finely shredded

Steam rice (see page 11) and set aside.

Heat half the oil in a wok, pour in the eggs and swirl around in the pan to make a thin omelette. When set underneath, turn and briefly cook the other side. Remove to a chopping board and cut into small pieces.

Reheat the wok with remaining oil over high heat. Stir-fry the garlic, spring onions, capsicum, dried shrimp and prawns (or chicken) for about 2 minutes, until cooked. Add pineapple and sauces, and stir-fry briefly. Add rice and eggs and stir-fry until combined. Stir in tofu at the last moment (if using). Add salt and pepper if needed. Garnish with chilli.

Glutinous Rice with Dried Shrimp & Mushrooms

Serves 4–6

2 cups glutinous white rice

2 pieces dried black cloud ear (wood ear) fungus

¾ cup raw peanuts

½ cup dried shrimp

½ cup diced Chinese roast pork

1 teaspoon salt

Soak the rice overnight in cold water. Pour boiling water over the fungus and soak for about 25 minutes. Drain.

Drain rice and mix with the peanuts. Spread evenly in a shallow heatproof dish. Place in a steamer and steam for about 20 minutes. Add dried shrimp, pork, mushrooms and salt, and mix well. Continue to cook until rice is tender (about 20 minutes). Alternatively, after adding the shrimp and pork, press the mixture into 4–6 small, greased heatproof dishes, cover with cling wrap and steam for about 20 minutes. Serve in the dish/es.

You can substitute Chinese roast duck, or Chinese sausage, for the pork.

Pad Thai with Chicken

Serves 3–5

350 g (12 oz) dried rice-stick noodles

1 tablespoon (15 g/½ oz) caster sugar

¼ cup (60 ml/2 fl oz) fish sauce

2 tablespoons (40 ml/1½ fl oz) tomato sauce

1 tablespoon (20 ml/¾ fl oz) sweet chilli sauce

120 g (4 oz) fresh bean sprouts

about 3 tablespoons (60 ml/2 fl oz) oil

2 eggs, well beaten

375 g (13 oz) chicken breast or thigh fillets, diced

1 spring onion, chopped

2 tablespoons chopped roasted peanuts

4 garlic chives, cut into 2.5-cm (1-in) lengths

lime or lemon wedges, to serve

Soak rice noodles in hot water for about 4 minutes, to soften. Tip into a colander to drain.

In a small bowl mix sugar with the fish, tomato and sweet chilli sauces. Set aside. Blanch bean sprouts in boiling water and drain.

Heat a wok and add 2 teaspoons of the oil. Pour in the eggs and swirl around in the pan to make a thin omelette. When set underneath, turn and briefly cook the other side. Remove to a chopping board and cut into small pieces.

Reheat the wok with the remaining oil and stir-fry the chicken and spring onion for several minutes until chicken is cooked. Pour in the mixed sauces and stir-fry briefly, then add the noodles and quickly toss over high heat. Add the omelette, bean sprouts, and half the peanuts and garlic chives, and toss until the noodles are coated with sauce.

Serve on a platter, scattered with remaining peanuts and garlic chives. Arrange lime or lemon wedges on the side.

Clay Pots with Prawns & Bean Threads

Serves 4

100 g (3½ oz) bean-thread noodles

2 tablespoons (40 ml/1½ fl oz) oil

3 spring onions (whites and half the greens), sliced

1½ teaspoons crushed ginger

1 teaspoon cracked black pepper

2 tablespoons (40 ml/1½ fl oz) oyster sauce

1 tablespoon (20 ml/¾ fl oz) fish sauce

2–3 teaspoons sugar

20 medium-sized raw (green) prawns, shelled and deveined but tails left on (remove heads if preferred)

8 cherry tomatoes, cut in half

Preheat the oven to 190°C (375°F).

Soak noodles in hot water for 10 minutes to soften, then drain well.

Heat oil in a wok and stir-fry the spring onions, ginger and pepper for 1 minute. Pour in the sauces, add sugar to taste and mix well. Add the prawns and tomatoes and toss until coated with the seasonings. Transfer to four small clay pots and add 2 tablespoons (40 ml/1½ fl oz) water to each pot. Cover and cook in the oven for about 10 minutes.

Fresh Rice Noodles with Broccolini & Pork

Serves 4

1 bunch broccolini (or use broccoli florets), cut into 4-cm (1½-in) lengths

2 tablespoons (40 ml/1½ fl oz) oil

250 g (9 oz) lean pork, cut into very thin slices

3 large cloves garlic, chopped

450 g (1 lb) fresh wide rice noodles, carefully separated

2 tablespoons (40 ml/1½ fl oz) fish sauce

2 tablespoons (40 ml/1½ fl oz) oyster sauce

freshly ground black pepper

sugar, to taste

CRISP-FRIED ONIONS

vegetable or peanut oil for frying

1 small red onion or 4 shallots, sliced

To make the crisp-fried onions, heat oil in a wok over medium heat and fry onion until crisp and golden-brown. Lift out and drain on paper towels.

Parboil broccolini for 3 minutes in lightly salted water. Drain well.

Heat a wok with the oil and stir-fry the pork until cooked (about 2 minutes). Remove to a plate.

Reheat the wok, adding a little more oil if needed, and stir-fry the garlic and noodles until noodles are coated with oil. (Do not overcook or stir too roughly, or noodles will break up.)

Return pork to the pan and add broccolini and fish sauce, 2 tablespoons (40 ml/1½ fl oz) water and half the oyster sauce. Stir-fry gently to combine.

Season with a little pepper and a few pinches of sugar. Serve on a platter, drizzled with remaining oyster sauce. Scatter with crisp-fried onions and serve.

ธ Wide rice noodles can be made by cutting rice-noodle sheets into strips.

Steamed Rice-noodle Rolls

2½ tablespoons (50 ml/ 1¾ fl oz) oil

3 cloves garlic, thinly sliced

1 fresh hot red chilli, deseeded and sliced

12 raw (green) prawns, shelled and deveined

150 g (5 oz) bean sprouts

2 spring onions, chopped

2–3 teaspoons fish sauce

500 g (1 lb 2 oz) fresh rice-noodle sheets

fresh coriander leaves, for garnish

dark soy sauce or oyster sauce, to serve

Heat oil in a wok and fry the garlic and chilli until crisp and brown. Remove with a slotted spoon and set aside.

Reheat the wok and stir-fry the prawns, bean sprouts and spring onions in the flavoured oil, until lightly cooked. Add fish sauce and stir-fry briefly. Set aside.

Cut each rice sheet into about six 15-cm (6-in) squares. Spoon some of the filling along the centre of each square, fold ends in, then roll up. Place in a steamer and steam for about 10 minutes.

Cut each roll into 3-cm (1¼-in) slices and transfer to a serving plate. Garnish with coriander leaves, a drizzle of dark soy or oyster sauce, and the fried garlic and chilli.

Crisp Rice Vermicelli with Sweet & Sour Sauce

Mee krob

Serves 4–6

- 4 tablespoons (60 g/3 oz) palm sugar or soft brown sugar
- 2 tablespoons (40 ml/1½ fl oz) freshly squeezed lime juice
- 2 teaspoons vinegar
- 1½ tablespoons (30 ml/1 fl oz) fish sauce
- 2 tablespoons (40 ml/1½ fl oz) tomato sauce
- 2 tablespoons (40 ml/1½ fl oz) sweet chilli sauce
- 180 g (6½ oz) dried rice vermicelli
- 2 eggs, lightly beaten
- oil for deep-frying
- 1 cup small peeled raw (green) prawns
- ½ cup diced firm tofu
- ½ cup diced chicken breast
- 3 garlic chives, chopped
- 2 tablespoons roasted peanuts, chopped
- 1 fresh hot red chilli, deseeded and finely shredded

In a small saucepan mix the sugar, lime juice, vinegar, fish sauce, tomato and sweet chilli sauces, and 3 tablespoons (60 ml/2 fl oz) water. Bring to the boil, then reduce heat and simmer for 2–3 minutes. Remove from the heat and let cool.

Break up the rice vermicelli, place in a bowl and add eggs, mixing well. >

Heat oil to 190°C (375°F) in a wok or large saucepan suitable for deep-frying. Fry the vermicelli in two batches – as soon as the pieces puff up, turn and cook the other side, then quickly remove and drain on paper towels.

Pour all but a few teaspoons oil from the wok. Reheat wok and stir-fry the prawns, tofu and chicken until cooked (about 2 minutes). Pour in the prepared sauce and mix well. Add fried noodles and very quickly toss in the sauce over high heat. (Do not cook for too long or they will soften.)

Pile the noodle mix onto a serving plate and garnish with garlic chives, peanuts and chilli.

Egg Noodles with Cabbage, Bean Sprouts & Mushrooms

Serves 3–4

250 g (9 oz) dried egg noodles

2 tablespoons (40 ml/1½ fl oz) oil

2½ cups chopped Chinese (or other) cabbage

8 fresh shiitake or Swiss brown mushrooms, quartered

2 spring onions, cut into 2.5-cm (1-in) lengths

4–5 thin slices fresh ginger, finely shredded

90 g (3 oz) fresh bean sprouts

1 teaspoon cornflour

¾ cup (180 ml/6 fl oz) mushroom stock or water

⅓ cup (80 ml/3 fl oz) oyster sauce

freshly ground black pepper

Place noodles in lightly salted boiling water and simmer for 4–6 minutes, until tender. Tip into a colander to drain.

Heat oil in a wok and stir-fry the cabbage, mushrooms, spring onions and ginger for about 2 minutes, until cabbage and mushrooms are tender. Add bean sprouts and stir-fry briefly, then add the drained noodles and mix well.

Stir cornflour into the stock or water and pour into the wok, along with half the oyster sauce and a generous grind of pepper. Stir over medium heat until the sauce thickens and becomes translucent (about 40 seconds). Serve on a platter, drizzled with the remaining oyster sauce.

ੴ Dried rice-stick noodles can replace the egg noodles.

Sweet Tastes

In Thailand you don't have to wait until after dinner to enjoy sweet tastes. Puddings, sweet drinks, desserts and cakes are eaten throughout the day, whether at home, in a restaurant or while shopping at a food market.

Thai desserts and sweets are full of surprising ingredients, like pumpkin, corn, tomatoes, sweet potato and water chestnuts. Some dishes use noodles, black rice or sticky rice. Many are flavoured with coconut, and bananas, mangoes and pineapple feature prominently.

Many sweet dishes can be prepared ahead of time, while others require just a few minutes of cooking. When time is short, a platter of fruit is a fine way to finish a spicy meal – Thais love fresh fruit and they often serve it elaborately carved.

< Lime Sago with Lychees & Mango (page 216)

Lime Sago with Lychees & Mango

Serves 4–6

1½ cups sago

salt

zest and juice of 2 limes

½ cup (110 g/ 4 oz) caster sugar

6–8 lychees, cut in half

1 mango cheek, finely diced

Mix sago with 4½ cups (1.1 L/2 pt 6 fl oz) water in a saucepan. Bring slowly to the boil, stirring. Add a large pinch of salt, reduce heat and simmer for 10–12 minutes, until sago is cooked and translucent. Stir in lime juice, zest and sugar, then set aside to cool for a few minutes.

Moisten four or six 150-ml (5-fl oz) jelly moulds with water and fill with the sago. Cover, and chill until firm.

Turn puddings out onto chilled plates and garnish with the lychees and mango.

You can use canned or frozen mango if fresh is unavailable.

Bananas Poached in Coconut Milk

Serves 4

2–3 tablespoons shredded coconut

4 large ripe bananas, cut into thick slices

½ cup (75 g/2½ oz) cornflour

800 ml (27 fl oz) coconut milk

4 tablespoons (60 g/3 oz) palm sugar

salt

Spread coconut in a small non-stick pan and toast over medium heat, stirring frequently, until golden-brown. Tip onto a plate to cool.

Coat banana slices with cornflour. Pour the coconut milk into a saucepan and add sugar and a few pinches of salt. Bring almost to the boil, then add bananas and simmer for about 4 minutes. Remove from the heat and set aside for 10 minutes.

Serve warm or well chilled, garnished with the toasted coconut.

Caramelised Fruit with Coconut Cream

Serves 4

2 tablespoons (30 g/1 oz) caster sugar

about ½ cup (60 g/3 oz) palm sugar

400 ml (13½ fl oz) coconut cream

2 tablespoons butter or nut oil (e.g. sunflower, peanut)

4 thick slices fresh or canned pineapple, cut in half

4 lady finger or other small bananas, cut in half lengthways

salt

In a small pan heat the caster sugar, without stirring, until it melts and turns golden-brown (it may harden to toffee). Quickly remove from the heat and add 3 tablespoons (60 ml/2 fl oz) water, allowing it to bubble up. Return pan to low heat and simmer until toffee melts, then add palm sugar and continue to simmer until dissolved. Add half the coconut cream and simmer over low heat for 1–2 minutes.

In a large non-stick pan heat the butter or oil, add the fruit and warm over high heat, turning once. Add the caramel syrup and simmer for a minute or two, to glaze the fruit.

Stir a pinch of salt into the remaining coconut cream. Serve the caramelised fruit with the coconut cream drizzled over.

Coconut Custard

Serves 6–8

¼ cup desiccated coconut

salt

400 ml (13½ fl oz) coconut
  cream

5 large eggs

½ cup (110 g/4 oz) caster
  sugar

Preheat the oven to 180°C (360°F). Grease 6–8 small (approximately 90-ml/3-fl oz) ovenproof cups or ramekins.

Spread coconut in a small non-stick pan and cook over medium heat, stirring frequently, until golden-brown. Tip onto a plate to cool.

Stir a small pinch of salt into the coconut cream. Whisk eggs and sugar together until creamy, then stir in coconut cream and toasted coconut.

Divide mixture between the cups and cover each with a piece of aluminium foil. Set in a baking dish half filled with warm water and bake for about 30 minutes. (Alternatively, you can steam them for about 18 minutes.)

Sticky Rice & Mango

Serves 6

1½ cups glutinous white rice

800 ml (27 fl oz) coconut cream

1 cup (220 g/8 oz) caster sugar

salt

2 large mangoes, sliced

Pour the rice into a bowl and cover with cold water. Leave overnight to soften and swell.

The next day, tip rice into a metal strainer and rinse under running cold water. Place the strainer over a saucepan of simmering water, cover with a lid or piece of aluminium foil to seal, and steam for about 25 minutes, until tender. Transfer to a bowl.

In a saucepan combine three-quarters of the coconut cream with the sugar and a few pinches of salt and simmer for about 8 minutes, stirring occasionally. Add to the bowl of rice and mix well. Cover and leave to cool.

Serve the sticky rice in bowls, garnished with mango and drizzled with remaining coconut cream.

Basil Seeds in Sweet Coconut Milk

Serves 4–6

1½ tablespoons dried sweet
  basil seeds

600 ml (20 fl oz) coconut milk,
  chilled

palm sugar or soft brown
  sugar, to taste

2–3 tablespoons fresh young
  coconut meat (optional)

Soak the basil seeds in cold water for about 5 hours – they will soften and develop a soft gelatinous layer around them. Drain well.

Sweeten the coconut milk with palm or soft brown sugar to taste, then divide between 4–6 glasses. Add a teaspoon of basil seeds and a few teaspoons of coconut meat (if using) to each glass. Serve chilled.

Dried sweet basil seeds and fresh coconut meat are available from Asian grocers.

Water Chestnut Gems in Iced Coconut Milk

Serves 6

¾ cup (170 g/6 oz) caster sugar

225 g (8 oz) water chestnuts, finely diced

red and green food colouring

½ cup (75 g/2½ oz) arrowroot or tapioca flour

375 ml (12½ fl oz) coconut milk

crushed ice, to serve

Combine sugar with 1½ cups (375 ml/12½ fl oz) water in a saucepan. Simmer for about 6 minutes, allow to cool, then refrigerate until cold.

Measure 4 teaspoons of cold water into each of two small bowls, then add enough food colouring to make one bright red and the other bright green. Add half the water chestnuts to each bowl and stir until they are well coloured. Set aside for 10 minutes, then drain and lightly rinse in cold water. Coat the water chestnuts with flour and tip into a colander, shaking off excess. Add to a pot of boiling water and simmer for a few minutes, until they float to the surface. Drain and cover with iced water to cool them quickly. Drain again.

Sweeten the coconut milk with the sugar syrup to taste, add the coloured 'gems' and serve over ice in tall glasses.

Rainbow-coloured tapioca is sold in Asian stores and can be cooked and used with, or instead of, the water chestnuts. Diced pineapple, young coconut meat, cooked sweet potato and sweet corn can also be added.

Pumpkin filled with Coconut Custard

Serves 6–8

1 × 1-kg (2 lb 3 oz) Jap pumpkin

salt

400 ml (13½ fl oz) coconut cream

3 large eggs

½ cup (110 g/4 oz) caster sugar

Preheat the oven to 180°C (360°F).

Wash the pumpkin and slice off the top. Scoop out the seeds and rinse the inside with lightly salted boiling water.

Stir a small pinch of salt into the coconut cream. Whisk eggs and sugar together until creamy, then stir in coconut cream.

Set the pumpkin in a steamer, pour in the custard and replace the top of the pumpkin. Steam gently for at least 35 minutes, until the pumpkin flesh is cooked but still holding its shape. Leave to cool completely at room temperature (or refrigerate) until custard and pumpkin are both firm enough to cut into wedges to serve.

Ginger Ice-cream

Serves 6

¼ cup stem ginger in syrup

1½ cups (375 ml/12½ fl oz) cream

1½ cups (375 ml/12½ fl oz) milk

5 egg yolks

¾ cup (170 g/6 oz) caster sugar

Purée the ginger and its syrup in a blender and set aside.

In a non-stick pan heat the cream and milk until mixture comes barely to the boil.

Whisk egg yolks with the sugar until pale and creamy and sugar is completely dissolved. Strain the cream and milk into the egg and sugar mixture and mix well. Pour back into the saucepan and place over low heat, or over a pan of simmering water. Cook very slowly until the mixture thickens enough to coat the back of a spoon. Remove from the heat and whisk slowly for a few minutes to arrest cooking. Let cool for 10–20 minutes, then stir in the ginger.

Churn mixture in an ice-cream maker until set.

Deep-fried Bananas

Serves 4–6

1 cup desiccated coconut

½ cup (75 g/2½ oz) rice flour

½ cup (75 g/2½ oz) self-raising flour

1 teaspoon salt

2 tablespoons (30 g/1 oz) caster sugar

oil for deep-frying

6 small bananas, cut in half lengthways

cinnamon sugar (optional)

Combine coconut, flours, salt and sugar in a bowl. Gradually add enough cold water to make a thick batter.

Heat oil to 190°C (375°F) in a wok or a large saucepan suitable for deep-frying. Cover a rack with paper towels, for draining.

When oil is slightly smoky, dip bananas into the batter to coat thickly, then deep-fry until golden-brown and floating on the surface. (For best results, cook bananas in two batches.)

Serve at once, sprinkled with cinnamon sugar if desired.

Mango Sorbet

¾ cup (170 g/6 oz) caster
   sugar

3 large mangoes, diced

1 egg white, lightly beaten

about 3 tablespoons (60 ml/
   2 fl oz) freshly squeezed
   lemon juice

Combine sugar with 1½ cups (375 ml/12½ fl oz) water in a saucepan. Simmer for about 6 minutes, then allow to cool completely (preferably chill in the refrigerator).

Place mangoes in a food processor and purée until smooth. Refrigerate until ready to use.

In ice-cream churn, combine the sugar syrup with 1½ cups (375 ml/ 12½ fl oz) of the mango purée and churn for 15 minutes. Add the egg white, and lemon juice to taste, then continue to churn until set.

Serve the sorbet drizzled with the remaining mango purée.

Extras

In Thailand, food is never dull. Alongside every meal are tiny dishes of spicy, sweet and salty sauces and relishes. Curry pastes, so essential to Thai cuisine, are vibrant compounds of herbs and spices, with pungent fermented seafood products underscoring the flavour. Although curry pastes can be bought, homemade pastes have a freshness and depth of flavour that's well worth the extra effort.

< Red Curry Paste (page 234)

Red Curry Paste

Makes enough for 2–4 curries

1 teaspoon toasted coriander seeds

½ teaspoon toasted cumin seeds

1 teaspoon black peppercorns

1 teaspoon dried chilli flakes

½ teaspoon shrimp paste

2 tablespoons chopped lemongrass

3 tablespoons chopped onion

2 teaspoons chopped galangal (or 1 teaspoon chopped fresh ginger)

1 tablespoon chopped garlic

3 tablespoons deseeded and chopped fresh red chillies

1–2 teaspoons ground sweet paprika (optional)

1–2 tablespoons oil

2 or 3 pinches salt

Combine all the ingredients in a spice grinder or blender, and grind to a smooth paste.

Use within two days. To keep longer, fry with an additional 1–2 tablespoons of oil for 1–2 minutes and store in the refrigerator in an airtight jar for up to 2 weeks.

Green Curry Paste

Makes enough for 2–3 curries

1 tablespoon chopped small
fresh green chillies

1 tablespoon chopped onion

1 tablespoon chopped garlic

1 tablespoon chopped
coriander stems and roots

3 teaspoons chopped galangal
(or 2 teaspoons chopped
fresh ginger)

1 teaspoon grated lime zest

1 teaspoon toasted coriander
seeds

½ teaspoon cracked black
pepper

½ teaspoon shrimp paste

1–2 tablespoons oil

2 or 3 pinches salt

Combine all the ingredients in a spice grinder or blender and grind to a smooth paste.

Use within two days. To keep longer, fry with an additional 1–2 tablespoons of oil for 1–2 minutes and store in the refrigerator in an airtight jar for up to 2 weeks.

Coconut Rice

Serves 4–6

800 ml (27 fl oz) coconut milk
1 teaspoon salt
1 teaspoon sugar
2¼ cups jasmine rice

Bring coconut milk to the boil in a saucepan and add the salt and sugar. Stir in rice and cover tightly. When liquid comes back to the boil, reduce heat to very low and cook gently, without lifting the lid, until rice is tender and coconut milk absorbed (about 15 minutes). Remove from heat and let stand, covered, for a further 10 minutes before serving.

Serve with curries or stir-fries, or as a side dish with salads.

Cucumber Relish

Makes about ¾ cup

2 tablespoons finely diced cucumber

1 tablespoon finely diced shallots or red onion

1 fresh hot red chilli, deseeded and chopped

⅓ cup (80 ml/3 fl oz) white vinegar or rice vinegar

2 tablespoons (30 g/1 oz) caster sugar

1–2 cloves garlic, finely chopped

2 teaspoons chopped fresh coriander leaves or finely shredded ginger

Combine cucumber, shallots (or onion) and chilli in a bowl.

In a small saucepan heat vinegar, sugar and 3–4 tablespoons water, stirring to dissolve sugar. Add garlic and coriander or ginger, remove from the heat and leave to cool.

Pour vinegar sauce over the cucumber and serve, or refrigerate for up to 4 days.

Peanut Dipping Sauce

Makes about ½ cup

2 tablespoons roasted peanuts

1 tablespoon dried shrimp

1 teaspoon grated fresh ginger

1½ teaspoons shrimp paste

about ½ cup (60 g/3 oz) palm sugar

Grind peanuts and dried shrimp to a coarse paste in a mortar and transfer to a small saucepan. Add remaining ingredients and 1¼ cups (310 ml/ 10½ fl oz) water and simmer for about 8 minutes, until reduced by half. Pour into a bowl to cool.

Serve at room temperature.

Satay Sauce

Makes about 2 cups

500 ml (17 fl oz) coconut milk

½ cup peanut butter

1½ tablespoons red curry
   paste (page 234)

1 tablespoon tamarind paste

3 tablespoons (45 g/2 oz)
   palm sugar

salt

In a small saucepan heat the coconut milk for about 5 minutes, until oil is
released and floats to the surface. Add the peanut butter and curry paste
and simmer for another 5 minutes, stirring. Season with the tamarind paste
and sugar, adjusting the amounts to taste, and add a pinch of salt. Cool to
room temperature.

Serve in shallow bowls, for dipping, or drizzled over cooked skewers.

Sweet Chilli Dipping Sauce

Makes about 1½ cups

2 tablespoons crushed chilli

1 cup (250 ml/8½ fl oz) rice
vinegar

2 teaspoons salt

3 teaspoons finely chopped
garlic

3 tablespoons (60 g/2 oz)
caster sugar, or to taste

Combine all ingredients in a small saucepan and simmer gently until well
reduced and syrupy (about 15 minutes), adding extra sugar if needed. Cool
before using.

Serve with spring rolls, cooked prawns or corn fritters.

Chilli–lime Dressing

Makes about ⅔ cup

2 tablespoons (40 ml/1½ fl oz) freshly squeezed lime juice

2 tablespoons (40 ml/1½ fl oz) rice vinegar

2 tablespoons (40 ml/1½ fl oz) fish sauce

1 tablespoon (15 g/¾ oz) palm sugar or soft brown sugar

1 tablespoon finely chopped fresh hot red chilli

½ teaspoon salt

Combine all the ingredients in a small saucepan. Heat almost to boiling, then pour into a bowl and let cool.

Crisp-fried Basil Leaves

Serves 4

**1–2 bunches fresh holy
  or sweet basil**
oil for deep-frying

Pluck larger basil leaves from the stems, then wash, drain and pat dry with paper towel.

Heat oil to 180°C (360°F) in a wok or a large pan suitable for deep-frying.

Place basil leaves in a frying basket and immerse in the oil – be careful, as they will splutter and splash. The leaves will cook quite quickly: shake the basket and if you hear the leaves 'rustle', they're ready. Remove the basket from the oil and tip leaves onto paper towels to drain. Use immediately.

These crispy leaves can be eaten on their own as a snack, or scattered over fried fish or vegetables, or grilled meat, as an elegant garnish.

Special Ingredients

BAMBOO SHOOTS These are available fresh or canned from supermarkets and Asian grocers. They have a distinctive, earthy flavour.

BAY PRAWNS Small prawns, also known as greentail prawns or greentail shrimp. They can be fried, whole and unshelled, and used as an alternative to dried shrimp.

BEAN-THREAD VERMICELLI Firm transparent noodles made from vegetable or mung bean starch. They are sold dried and must be soaked before use.

BLACK CLOUD EAR (WOOD EAR) FUNGUS A frilly black fungus that is usually sold dried and needs to be soaked before use. It has a mild flavour and slightly crunchy texture. It is available from Asian grocers.

CHILLI BEAN PASTE Salted soybeans mashed with chilli and salt. Used as a richly flavoured seasoning in stir-fries, rice dishes and braises. It is sold in Asian groceries.

CHINESE SAUSAGE (THAI *KUN CHIANG*) This dried, aromatic pork sausage is also known by its Chinese name, *lap cheong*. It is available from supermarkets and Asian food stores.

COCONUT Used in myriad ways in Thai cooking. The flesh of ripe coconuts is grated and squeezed to extract coconut cream, which in turn is infused with water to produce coconut milk. Canned coconut cream and milk are ready to use, while powdered coconut is mixed with warm water to make cream or milk. Desiccated and shredded coconut add texture to desserts and salads. Fresh young coconut meat adds its own unique texture to sweet dishes.

DRIED SHRIMP These small shrimps are used in many Asian cuisines, imparting a unique flavour.

EGG NOODLES Made with wheat flour and egg, these noodles can be bought dried or fresh.

EGGPLANTS (ASIAN) These come in many shapes, sizes and colours. Thai pea eggplants are a green pea-sized variety. *Makhua khun* eggplants are walnut-sized. There are also white, green and purple eggplants the size of a golf ball, and others that are long and slender. The familiar large globe eggplant is often used as well. Check your local Asian grocer to see what's available.

ENOKI MUSHROOMS Long, thin white mushrooms with a mild flavour. They are available canned, but are better fresh.

FISH SAUCE Fish sauce is to Thai cooking what soy sauce is to Chinese food. It adds salty flavour to curries, stir-fries, sauces and dressings, but also accentuates the flavours of other ingredients.

GALANGAL Resembles fresh root ginger, but has a harder, woodier texture, for which reason it is only used as a seasoning and not eaten. Fresh galangal can be found in Asian food stores, but dried and ground galangal can be used instead in curry sauces and pastes. Fresh ginger is another alternative, but as its flavour is stronger, use half the quantity.

GLUTINOUS WHITE RICE A short-grain rice that has a gooey consistency when cooked. It is used to make sticky rice and sweet dishes.

KAFFIR LIME Different to the common Tahitian lime, this lime has a unique, intense fragrance. The zest can be used in strips or grated, while the leaves are used whole, torn or finely shredded as a seasoning or garnish. Buy fresh or frozen, rather than dried. Fresh leaves keep for several weeks.

LEMONGRASS The stem of this herb has a fragrant lemony flavour. Only the lower 15 cm (6 in) is used: before use, trim off the top and bottom of the stem and discard the outer layers if they are dry and coarse; slitting and bruising the stem helps release the wonderful flavour. Available in supermarkets and Asian stores, lemongrass can be stored for several weeks in the fridge.

OYSTER SAUCE A thick, dark-brown sauce made from oysters, which has a strong salty flavour and is used in stir-fries and braised dishes. (Vegetarian versions are available.)

PALM SUGAR May be derived from sugar, sago or coconut palms. Like cane sugar it varies from pale to dark: the darker the colour, the stronger the flavour. Light palm sugar is used for pale sauces and dressings, and dark for braising and when more intense flavour and colour are needed. It comes in jars, blocks and logs. Soft brown sugar can be substituted.

RICE NOODLES There are a number of varieties: dried rice sticks, dried rice vermicelli, and fresh rice noodles or sheets. Dried noodles are soaked before use. Fresh rice noodles are used straight from the pack (or, if oily, rinsed quickly with hot water before use) and will keep for 2–4 days after opening. Do not overcook fresh noodles or they will fall apart.

SHIITAKE MUSHROOMS Used in many Asian cuisines, these mushrooms have a meaty flavour and are available dried or fresh.

SHRIMP PASTE A foul-smelling ingredient made from fermented, ground shrimps. It is used to enliven other flavours, while adding its own complex and salty taste. It is sold as compressed blocks, a solid paste or a soft pink-grey paste in a jar. Dry-roast dried shrimp paste in a foil parcel before using.

STRAW MUSHROOMS Mild in flavour, these mushrooms are available canned, and occasionally fresh.

TAMARIND PASTE Adds a tart–sour flavour to dishes, and is also used to tenderise meat. Lemon juice can be used as a substitute.

TOFU Coagulated soy milk, available fresh or processed. It is also known as beancurd. A number of varieties is available: firm, soft, silken and fried.

WATER SPINACH A spinach-like vegetable that is becoming more available. You can use English spinach or watercress instead.

Conversions

(Note: all conversions are approximate)

Important note: All cup and spoon measures given in this book are based on Australian standards. The most important thing to remember is that an Australian cup = 250 ml, while an American cup = 237 ml and a British cup = 284 ml. Also, an Australian tablespoon is equivalent to 4 teaspoons, not 3 teaspoons as in the United States and Britain. US equivalents have been provided throughout for all liquid cup/spoon measures. Equivalents for dry ingredients measured in cups/spoons have been included for flour, sugar and rising agents such as baking powder. For other dry ingredients (chopped vegetables, nuts, etc.), American cooks should be generous with their cup measures – slight variations in quantities of such ingredients are unlikely to affect results.

VOLUME

Australian cups/spoons	Millilitres	US fluid ounces
*1 teaspoon	5 ml	
1 tablespoon (4 teaspoons)	20 ml	¾ fl oz
1½ tablespoons	30 ml	1 fl oz
2 tablespoons	40 ml	1½ fl oz
¼ cup	60 ml	2 fl oz
⅓ cup	80 ml	3 fl oz
½ cup	125 ml	4 fl oz
¾ cup	180 ml	6 fl oz
1 cup	250 ml	8½ fl oz
4 cups	1 L	34 fl oz

*the volume of a teaspoon is the same around the world

SIZE

Centimetres	Inches
1 cm	⅜ in
2 cm	¾ in
2.5 cm	1 in
5 cm	2 in
10 cm	4 in
15 cm	6 in
20 cm	8 in
30 cm	12 in

TEMPERATURE

Celsius	Fahrenheit
150°C	300°F
160°C	320°F
170°C	340°F
180°C	360°F
190°C	375°F
200°C	390°F
210°C	410°F
220°C	420°F

WEIGHT

Grams	Ounces
15 g	½ oz
30 g	1 oz
60 g	2 oz
85 g	3 oz
110 g	4 oz
140 g	5 oz
170 g	6 oz
200 g	7 oz
225 g	8 oz (½ lb)
450 g	16 oz (1 lb)
500 g	1 lb 2 oz
900 g	2 lb
1 kg	2 lb 3 oz

Index

LONDON, NEW YORK, MUNICH,
MELBOURNE and DELHI

First published in Great Britain in 2011 by
Dorling Kindersley, 80 Strand, London, WC2R 0RL

A Penguin Company

Published by Penguin Group (Australia), 2010
250 Camberwell Road, Camberwell, Victoria 3124, Australia
(a division of Pearson Australia Group Pty Ltd)

10 9 8 7 6 5 4 3 2 1

Design by Claire Tice and Marley Flory © Penguin Group (Australia)
Photography by Julie Renouf
Food styling by Lee Blaylock
Typeset in Nimbus Sans Novus by Post Pre-press Group, Brisbane, Queensland
Scanning and separations by Splitting Image P/L, Clayton, Victoria
Printed and bound in China by Everbest Printing Co. Ltd

A CIP catalogue record for this book is available from the British Library.

ISBN: 978-1-4053-6323-5

Discover more at www.dk.com